101 healthy Vegan Burgers Recipes

Quick & Easy Grilled, Fried, Baked Vegan Recipes

Nadav Daniel

101 vegan burger, Copyright@2013 by Nadav Daniel. All rights reserved. No part of this book may be used or reproduced in any matter whatsoever without permission in writing from the author except in the case of brief quotations embodied in critical articles or review

DISCLAIMER:

The information presented in this book represents the views of the publisher as of the date of publication. The publisher reserves the rights to alter and update their opinions based on new conditions. This report is for informational purposes only. The author and publisher do not accept any responsibilities for any liabilities resulting from the use of this information. While every attempt has been made to verify the information provided here, the author and the publisher cannot assume any responsibility for errors, inaccuracies or omissions.

Any similarities with people or facts are unintentional

Dedication

To all of the amazing members of the vegan comunity who shared with me their unique and delicious recipes. In my opinion, this collection of recipes is a wonderful proof of the unique mutual support shared by vegans worldwide

Table of Contents

Introduction 7
First of all - A wonderful recipe for an amazing and healthy vegan burger buns!! 9
Chapter 1: Grilled Vegan Burgers 10
    Black Lentil and Oatmeal Burgers 11
    Sesame Seed Bean Burgers 12
    Caribbean Portobello Burgers 13
    Grilled Eggplant and Pesto Burgers 14
    Curry Cauliflower Burgers 15
    Black Bean and Oatmeal Burgers 16
    Broccoli and Green Pea Vegan Burgers 17
    Lentil and Pea Burgers 18
    Balsamic Portobello Burgers 19
    Curry and Chickpea Burgers 20
    Potato Veggie Burgers 21
    Mushroom and Bean Burgers 22
    Kidney Bean and Spinach Burgers 23
    Curried Eggplant and Tomato Burgers 24
    Portobello Burgers 25
    Grilled Black Bean and Broccoli Burgers 26
    Simple Zucchini Burgers 27
    Sweet Potato Grilled Burgers 28
    Grilled Tofu and Portobello Burgers 29
    Pineapple and Mushroom Burgers 30
    Bulgur and Chickpeas Burgers 31
    Roasted Bell Pepper and Quinoa Burgers 32
    Roasted Onion and Portobello Burgers 33
    Tropical Black Bean Burgers 34
    Almond and Tofu Burgers 35
    Broccoli and Mushroom Grilled Burgers 36
    Sweet Corn and Sweet Potato Burgers 37
    Spicy Thai Vegan Burger 38
    Yellow Squash Burgers 39
    Buckwheat and Grilled Pineapple Burgers 40
    Leek and Broccoli Burgers 41
    Soybean and Pecan Burgers 42
    Tofu and Onion Marmalade Burgers 43
    Spinach and Pistachio Burgers 44
Chapter 2: Fried Burgers 45

Pinto Burgers with Chipotle Aioli...46
Fennel and Beetroot Burger 47
Curried Mushroom Burgers 48
Chickpea and Sweet Corn Burgers...49
Fried Potato and Garlic Burgers...50
Broccoli and Pistachio Spicy Burgers..51
Beet and Quinoa Black Bean Burgers..52
Chipotle Black Bean Burgers...53
Carrot and Parsnip Burgers..54
Curry and Chickpea Burgers..55
Curried Vegetable Burgers...56
Spicy Quinoa Burgers..57
Zucchini Fried Burgers..58
Peanut Butter Chickpea Burgers..59
Eggplant and Cumin Burgers...60
Garlic Potato Burgers...61
Eggplant and Cauliflower Fried Burgers 62
Okra Burgers..63
Walnut and Brown Rice Vegan Burgers..64
Black Bean Burgers with Lime Dressing...65
Beet and Black Bean Fried Burger...66
Cauliflower and Green Pea Burgers...67
Cilantro Bean Burgers with Spicy Guacamole..68
Pumpkin and Cumin Flavored Burgers...69
Green Lentil and Almond Burgers...70
Mediterranean Burgers...71
Pecan and Mushroom Burgers...72
Soybean Burgers..73
Roasted Bell Pepper and Lentil Burgers..74
Zucchini and Carrot Burgers..75
Sweet Potato and Basil Burgers...76
Sun-dried Tomatoes and Black Bean Burgers...77
Spicy Spinach and Tofu Burgers..78
Chapter 3: Baked Burgers...79
Sweet Potato and Parsley Burgers..80
Basil and Quinoa Burgers..81
Stuffed Portobello Burgers with Onion Marmalade......................................82
Bulgur and Parsley Baked Burgers..83
Spinach Tofu Burgers..84
Baked Sweet Corn Tofu Burgers 85
Herbed Tofu Burger...86
Spicy Mushroom and Black-eyed Pea Burgers..87
Vegetable Flax Seed Burgers...88

Carrot and Walnut Burgers 89
Sesame Seeds and Millet Burgers 90
Brown Lentil and Nut Burgers 91
Baked Falafel Burgers 92
Lentil and Pesto Burgers 93
Smoky Beetroot Burgers 94
Pumpkin Black Beans Burgers 95
Kale and Oatmeal Burgers 96
Green Lentils and Sunflower Seed Burgers with Garlic Sauce 97
Baked Sesame Tofu Burgers 98
Roasted Red Pepper and Eggplant Burgers 99
Oatmeal and Beetroot Burgers with Barley Salad 100
Potato and Bean Burgers with Garlic Aioli 101
Courgette Burgers 102
Crispy Chickpea Burgers 103
Broccoli and Lentil Baked Burgers 104
Tofu Tempeh Burger 105
Tabbouleh Burgers 106
Cauliflower and Broccoli Burgers 107
Fava Bean Burgers 108
Leek and Cauliflower Burgers 109
Baked Garlic and Bean Burgers 110
Chickpea and Tempeh Burgers 111
Tofu Stuffed Mushrooms Burgers 112
Lentil, Bean and Coriander Burgers 113
Summary 114
ABOUT THE AUTHOR 115

Introduction

     Congratulations on making a smart purchase in buying this one of a kind, unique book—101 healthy vegan burgers!! I'm so proud of this book because this is the first collection of vegan burgers that was ever written—a great substitute for animal burgers or veggie burgers. With this purchase you have chosen to step forward to the prospect of a wonderful life, harmonious with nature by eating vegan! Not everyone chooses to make the big change and the important transition into the world of veganism and, for that, I applaud you ! Now you are going to be exposed to the world of 101 tasty, creative and delicious vegan burger recipes.

 Veganism is a wonderful world and I know if you persist in preparing vegan burgers you will raise the quality of your life and that of your family. There is no doubt that consuming vegan recipes is a great way to a surge of joy, energy, vigor and strength—physical health leads to a healthy mind.

It has been scientifically proven that vegan diets are the healthiest choice for the human body. A recent study shows that plant-based diets either minimize or completely eliminate people's genetic propensity to develop chronic diseases, such as diabetes type 2, cardiovascular disease and cancer. It is also known that a vegan diet promotes long lasting weight loss and increases energy!

But here it is important to note that, even with an awareness of the physical problems and the serious ethical nature of eating burgers, vegans nonetheless have challenging situations ... If you are vegan, like me, you're probably familiar with situations wherein family or friends are sitting in a garden, having a barbecue or a family meal, and you only have a salad ... I always fantasized at these events, that I make a delicious,juicy and healthy burgers for me and my family. Then one day I thought, *it would be great to have a recipe book that includes all types of vegan burgers.* I knew there are plenty of veggie burger recipe books, but I couldn't find one about vegan burgers. It was then I decided to undertake in-depth research to write the wonderful book now in your hands!

I come from a background of cooking (for many years I worked in different kitchens in my country), but I felt that I needed some help to make the complete vegan burger book recipes. So I decided to contact members of our worldwide community through forums for vegans. I asked for recipes and tips and the response was amazing! I decided to find the ultimate solutions for our community and began to write books of wonderful recipes for food that I personally like the most...

My study intended to show that there are dozens of ways to prepare tasty and healthy burgers while using only products from nature. Veggie burgers—your little brother came to town!

And now we go out together on a fascinating journey of changing eating habits in our families' and the most popular dish in the United States. You will feel very creative, because the recipes are so healthy, juicy and varied. I know that as soon as vegans prepare these burgers at a barbecue with friends, their friends will also want to taste them—because when they pass out from fatigue, you will have energy and a sense of alertness. In this way, you will project happiness which hopefully, will affect those around you!

Just before we jump into the water and start the change, I just want to say thanks to all of the amazing people who shared with me their unique and delicious recipes. In my opinion, this collection of recipes is a wonderful proof of the unique mutual support shared by vegans worldwide. My belief is that we all, together, can really make a difference in the world. And, of course, I want to say, once again, thank you for purchasing "101 healthy vegan burgers" and I wish us all a fascinating learning process—tasty, healthy and nutritious! Let's get going!

First of all - A wonderful recipe for an amazing and healthy vegan burger buns!!

Serving:
14-16 vegan burger buns

Ingredients:
2 cups of Spelt flour
1 teaspoon salt
2 teaspoons of dry yeast
¼ cup sugar
Cup and a half of water

Directions:
1. Knead the dough (not too much kneading) and of course you can knead it in a mixer or by hand. Bloat when the dough is covered, until the volume of the dough is doubled. Divide the dough into 16 pieces and form hamburger buns, puff on a pan lined with baking paper.
2. Meanwhile, heat oven to 240, put a little pattern with boiling water at the bottom of the oven, seal each bun and bake 18-20 minutes. Wait until they get cold (if you can, the smell usually will not allow...) and enjoy the beautiful and delicious buns!

Chapter 1: Grilled Vegan Burgers

Vegan burgers are just as good as non-vegetarian ones and, may I add, much healthier (packed with fiber and vitamins). There are various options for cooking them, but somohow grilling is the option that most people prefer.

Cooking them on the grill is proven to be much healthier. Plus, grilling the burgers enhances their natural flavors, while adding a mild, smoky aroma we all love. The vegetables release their flavors slowly and steadily and the burgers are not at risk of overcooking, or losing their nutrients and vitamins.

This category includes grilled burger recipes, healthy and delicious options for people who enjoy the vegan lifestyle and want to try new ways of cooking their food.

<u>Black Lentil and Oatmeal Burgers</u>

Lentils are known for their high fiber content and they are great in this recipe because they're filling and nutritious.

Servings: 4-6 burgers

Ingredients:
1 1/2 cup uncooked black lentils
1 cup brown rice
1 small onion, finely chopped
1 carrot, peeled and finely grated
2 garlic cloves, minced
1 cup uncooked oatmeal
Salt, pepper
2 tablespoons freshly chopped parsley

Directions:
1. Pour 5 cups of water into a large pot and bring to a boil. Add a pinch of salt and stir in the rice. Cook for 20 minutes then add the lentils and oatmeal and cook for another 20 minutes. Remove from heat and allow to cool.
2. Transfer the lentils and rice to a bowl and stir in the chopped onion, carrot and garlic, and adjust the taste with salt and pepper. Mix in the chopped parsley and shape into burgers with damp hands.
3. Heat a grill pan and brush it with olive oil. Cook the burgers on both sides until golden brown. It will take 5-6 minutes per side.
4. Serve between 2 slices of bread or on a burger bun with a few tomato slices and a lettuce leaf if you prefer.

Sesame Seed Bean Burgers

Beans are highly nutritional and tasty, so using them to make burgers seems like a good idea, especially if you add other delicious and fragrant ingredients, such as garlic and cayenne pepper.

Servings: 8-10 burgers

Ingredients:
2 cups canned black beans, drained
2 cups canned white beans, drained
1/3 cup uncooked oatmeal
1 carrot, peeled and sliced
2 tablespoons olive oil
1 teaspoon cumin powder
4 garlic cloves, minced
1 teaspoon onion powder
1/4 teaspoon cayenne pepper
Salt, freshly ground pepper
1/2 cup sesame seeds

Directions:
1. Put the oatmeal and carrots in a food processor and pulse a few times until ground. Add the beans, olive oil, onion powder, cumin, garlic, cayenne pepper, and salt to taste. Pulse until a smooth paste forms.
2. Wet your hands and form burgers. Roll each of them through sesame seeds and place aside.
3. Heat a grill pan over a medium flame and brush it with a bit of olive oil. Cook the burgers on both sides in the pan until golden brown. Serve between 2 slices of bread or on a burger bun with a few red onion rings and fresh lettuce leaves.

Caribbean Portobello Burgers

Tangy but sweet, with a unique flavor that not everyone might like, these burgers combine the taste of grilled pineapples with earthy mushrooms to create a delicious, easy burger, perfect for any party.

Servings: 2-4 burgers

Ingredients:
2 Portobello mushrooms
2 slices fresh pineapple
1 teaspoon dried thyme
1 teaspoon honey
1 teaspoon soy sauce
Salt, pepper
Vegan burger buns
Arugula for serving

Directions:
1. In a small bowl, mix together the soy sauce and honey. Brush the pineapple slices with this mixture.
2. Heat a grill pan over a medium flame and brush it with a bit of vegetable oil.
3. Grill the pineapple slices on each side until browned.
4. Remove from the pan and cook the mushrooms in the same pan for a few minutes, seasoning them with just a pinch of salt and freshly ground pepper.
5. Serve the mushrooms and pineapple layered on vegan burger buns with arugula as garnish.

Grilled Eggplant and Pesto Burgers

Pesto is an Italian aromatic sauce and, although it has a strong basil taste, it is not at all overwhelming, especially paired with the mild eggplant.

Servings: 4 burgers

Ingredients:

2 small eggplants, cut into 1/2 inch thick slices
3 tablespoons olive oil
3 tablespoons balsamic vinegar
1 teaspoon dried basil
1 teaspoon dried oregano
4 medium size Vegan burger buns
4 tomato slices
4 lettuce leaves
Salt, pepper

For the pesto:
1 cup packed basil leaves
1/2 cup pine nuts
4 tablespoons olive oil
1 teaspoon lemon juice
Salt, pepper

Directions:

1. Put the eggplant slices in a sieve and sprinkle plenty of salt over it. Let it stand like that for 30 minutes. This process helps extract the natural bitterness of the eggplant. After 30 minutes, rinse the slices and drain them on paper towels.
2. Heat a grill pan on a medium flame. Brush each eggplant slice with olive oil then cook them on the grill on both sides for 6-7 minutes until they are soft.
3. In the meantime, whisk the balsamic vinegar with the dried basil and oregano in a bowl. When the eggplant slices are cooked, put them in the bowl to marinade and leave them there while you prepare the rest of the ingredients.
4. Now we are ready for the pesto: Put the basil leaves, pine nuts and lemon juice in a small blender or food processor and pulse, adding the olive oil gradually. Blend until smooth.
5. Slice the vegan burger buns in half lengthwise and spread pesto sauce on the bottom side of the bun. Top with an eggplant slice, followed by a tomato slice and a lettuce leaf. Serve immediately, although it is just as good a few hours later after the eggplant has marinated more.

Curry Cauliflower Burgers

Similar to broccoli, cauliflower has a mild taste but it works great with curry as they enhance each other's tastes. Plus, cauliflower is also very healthy and nutritious and that is reason enough to include it in your diet.

Servings: 4-6 burgers

Ingredients:
1 head cauliflower, trimmed and cut into florets
1 teaspoon curry
2 tablespoons tahini paste
1/2 cup breadcrumbs
2 tablespoons chopped chives
2 tablespoons sunflower seeds
Salt, pepper

Directions:
1. Put the cauliflower florets into a steamer and cook them for 15-20 minutes or until tender. Transfer into a bowl and mash them with a potato masher. They don't have to be puréed completely. Stir in the tahini paste, curry and breadcrumbs, followed by the chopped chives and sunflower seeds. Adjust the taste with salt and pepper and form small patties. Set them aside.
2. Heat a grill pan and brush it with a bit of oil, then grill the burgers on each side for 5-6 minutes until just slightly browned.
3. Serve on vegan burger buns with your favorite toppings.

Black Bean and Oatmeal Burgers

Filling and easy to make, these burgers will be a delight for your senses. Spicy, but not too spicy, they are simply delicious.

Servings: 8-10 burgers

Ingredients:
3 cups canned black beans, drained and rinsed
1 cup mushrooms, diced
2/3 cup rolled oats
3 garlic cloves
1 teaspoon cumin seeds
4 tablespoons sesame seeds
2 tablespoons vegetable oil
Salt, pepper
Multigrain Vegan burger buns
Spicy mustard
Tomato slices and baby spinach for serving

Directions:
1. Put half of the beans in a food processor or blender and stir in the mushrooms, garlic, cumin seeds and a pinch of pepper and salt. Purée them together until smooth. Transfer the mixture into a bowl and stir in the remaining beans and rolled oats.
2. Wet your hands and form small burgers. Coat each one in sesame seeds and set them aside.
3. Heat a grilling pan over a medium flame and brush it with vegetable oil.
4. Cook every burger on each side for 6-7 minutes until cooked through and slightly browned at the edges. Serve on vegan burger buns with spicy mustard, tomato slices and baby spinach leaves.

Broccoli and Green Pea Vegan Burgers

Broccoli and green peas are both green vegetables and they taste somehow similar, but, in this burger, they somehow enhance each other's tastes. Plus, these burgers are a great way to trick your kids into eating their green vegetables

Servings: 4-6 burgers

Ingredients:
1 broccoli head, cut into florets
1 cup canned cooked green peas
1 teaspoon cumin powder
1/2 teaspoon garlic powder
Salt, pepper
Vegan burger buns
Tomatoes

Directions:
1. Pour a few cups of water in a large pot and bring to a boil. Add a pinch of salt and throw in the broccoli. Cook for 4-5 minutes then strain. Set aside to cool.
2. Mix the broccoli, green peas, cumin powder, garlic powder, freshly ground pepper and salt in a food processor. Pulse a few times until a smooth paste forms. Wet your hands and form burgers.
3. Heat a grill pan over a medium flame and cook them on both sides until golden brown. Serve them on vegan burger buns with tomato slices. Enjoy!

Lentil and Pea Burgers

Both lentils and peas are delicious and they make an excellent burger for all those embracing the vegan lifestyle.

Servings: 6-8 burgers

Ingredients:
3 cups canned lentils, drained
1 cup cooked peas
1 cup sweet potatoes, cooked
1/2 cup oatmeal
1 teaspoon lemon juice
1 teaspoon soy sauce
1/4 teaspoon cayenne pepper
1 teaspoon garlic powder
1 teaspoon onion powder
Salt, pepper

Directions:

1. Put the lentils and cooked peas in a food processor and pulse a few times until ground. Add the potatoes and oatmeal and pulse until they transform into a paste.
2. Stir in the lemon juice, soy sauce, cayenne pepper, garlic powder and onion powder. Adjust the taste with salt and pepper and form burgers with wet hands to prevent them from sticking
3. Heat a grill pan on a medium flame. Brush the pan with olive oil, or another vegetable oil, and cook the burgers on both sides until golden brown.
4. Serve on vegan burger buns with tomato slices, lettuce and fresh parsley for an intense flavor. Enjoy!

Balsamic Portobello Burgers

Easy to do, but delicious and healthy, these burgers are light enough to be either lunch or dinner.

Servings: 2 burgers

Ingredients:
2 Portobello mushrooms
2 tablespoons balsamic vinegar
2 tablespoons chopped parsley
Salt, pepper
Vegan burger buns, tomato slices, lettuce leaves

Directions:
1. Season the mushrooms with salt and pepper and brush them with oil.
2. Heat a grill pan on a medium flame and cook the mushrooms on each side for 4-5 minutes until cooked through. Remove from heat. In a bowl, pour in the balsamic vinegar and sprinkle the parsley. Toss to evenly coat.
3. Serve the mushrooms on vegan burger buns with tomato slices and lettuce leaves.

Curry and Chickpea Burgers

Chickpeas are so versatile. They are used to make soups, stews, and why not, even burgers. They are healthy and have a high fiber content, which makes them perfect for any meal.

Servings: 4-6 burgers

Ingredients:
2 cups canned chickpeas
3 garlic cloves, minced
2 tablespoons olive oil
1 teaspoon cumin
1 teaspoon curry powder
1/4 teaspoon cayenne pepper
1 tablespoon rice flour
2 tablespoons chopped coriander
Salt, pepper to taste

Directions:
4. Put the chickpeas into a food processor and pulse a few times until a paste forms. Stir in the garlic, curry powder, cumin and cayenne. Adjust the taste with enough salt and pepper then add the chopped coriander. Wet your hands slightly, take spoons of mixture and give them the classic burger shape.
5. Heat a grill pan on a medium flame and cook the burgers on one side for 5-6 minutes and then flip them over gently and keep cooking for 5 more minutes until golden brown on both sides. Serve between two slices of bread, or on vegan burger buns, along with tomato slices and cucumber or lettuce leaves.
6. Additionally, you can make a vegan yogurt and dill sauce by mixing 1/2 cup almond yogurt with 2 tablespoons freshly chopped dill. Spread this sauce over the burgers and serve as soon as possible for an enhanced taste

Potato Veggie Burgers

Apart from the usual cooking of potatoes into mash and fries, you can also try these burgers. They are fairly easy to make, but delicious and filling.

Servings: 4-6 burgers

Ingredients:
1 1/2 cup canned white beans
1 small carrot, grated
1 green onion, finely chopped
4 potatoes, grated
1/2 cup corn
Salt, pepper
2 tablespoons fresh parsley

Directions:
1. Put the beans in a blender and puree until a smooth paste forms. Transfer into a bowl and add the potatoes, carrot, green onion, corn, parsley and salt and pepper to taste.
2. Wet your hands and form burgers. Heat a grill pan on a medium flame and brush it with olive oil. Cook the burgers on both sides 6-7 minutes.
3. Serve them warm with a vegan yogurt and garlic sauce if you like.

Mushroom and Bean Burgers

Mushrooms' taste and texture is very similar to meat when cooked so you won't even be able to tell the difference in this burger.

Servings: 4-6 burgers

Ingredients:
1 1/2 cup fresh chopped mushrooms
2 garlic cloves, minced
1 cup canned white beans
1 tablespoon chopped parsley
2 green onions, chopped
1/4 teaspoon cumin powder
Salt, pepper

Directions:
1. Using a fork, mash the beans until a smooth paste forms. You can also purée them in a blender or food processor. Transfer the beans into a bowl and stir in the green onion, garlic, chopped mushrooms, cumin powder, parsley and salt and pepper to taste.
2. Wet your hands and form burgers.
3. Heat a grill pan on a medium flame and cook the burgers on both sides for 7-8 minutes until golden brown and cooked through.

Kidney Bean and Spinach Burgers

Vegan burgers can pretty much contain any combination of vegetables as long as they work together. This recipe includes kidney beans and spinach and the burgers are grilled for a slightly smoky taste to enhance all the flavors.

Servings: 8-10 burgers

Ingredients:
3 cups canned kidney beans
3/4 cup rolled oats
1/2 teaspoon tamarind paste
2 garlic cloves, minced
1/2 small onion, chopped
1 cup baby spinach leaves, chopped
1 teaspoon nutritional yeast
1/2 cup pumpkin seeds
1/4 teaspoon chili powder
Vegan burger buns and tomato slices for serving
Salt, pepper

Directions:
1. Put the kidney beans in a food processor or blender and pulse until a smooth paste forms. Transfer into a bowl and stir in the rolled oats, tamarind paste, garlic, chopped onion, yeast, pumpkin seeds, chili powder and spinach leaves. Adjust the taste with a pinch of salt and pepper.
2. Wet or grease your hands and take spoonfuls of mixture and form burgers. Set them aside.
3. Heat a grill pan on a medium flame and brush it with a bit of vegetable oil. Cook the burgers on both sides 6-7 minutes until golden brown and cooked through. Serve them warm on a burger bun, topped with a tomato slice.

Curried Eggplant and Tomato Burgers

Nutritious and filling, these burgers bring to the table a lovely curried, smoky flavor that the audience will simply love.

Servings: 4 burgers

Ingredients:
1 eggplant, sliced
2 large tomato, cut in thick slices
2 tablespoons balsamic vinegar
2 tablespoons olive oil
1/2 teaspoon dried basil
Salt, pepper
Vegan burger buns

Directions:
1. Put the eggplant and tomato in a colander and sprinkle plenty of salt. Let them rest for 30 minutes then rinse and drain on paper towels.
2. Mix the vinegar with olive oil in a small bowl and brush the eggplant slices.
3. Heat a grill pan over a medium flame then cook the eggplant slices on each side for a few minutes until tender. Remove from the pan and cook the tomato slices in the same pan.
4. Serve the eggplant and tomatoes layered on vegan burger buns.

Portobello Burgers

Portobello are a kind of mushroom that is perfect for grilling because of their incredibly large size but they are also delicious, especially if marinated.

Servings: 2 burgers

Ingredients:
2 large Portobello mushrooms
1/4 cup balsamic vinegar
2 tablespoons extra virgin olive oil
1 garlic clove, minced
1 teaspoon dried basil
Salt, pepper

Directions:
1. In a large bowl, mix together the vinegar with olive oil, minced garlic and basil. Add a pinch of salt and freshly ground pepper and put the mushrooms into the sauce. Let them marinade for 30 minutes.
2. Heat a grill pan on a medium flame and brush it with olive oil. Put the mushrooms on the grill and cook them on both sides until golden brown.
3. Serve them warm on vegan burger buns with tomato slices and onion rings

Grilled Black Bean and Broccoli Burgers

Not many people like broccoli so it is a good idea to hide it in food that has other main ingredients, such as these delicious black bean burgers.

Servings: 4-6 burgers

Ingredients:
1 1/2 cups canned black beans
1 red bell pepper, cored and chopped
2 green onions
1/2 cup wheat germ
2 garlic cloves, minced
1/2 cup chopped walnuts
1/2 cup pumpkin seeds
1 teaspoon nutritional yeast
1/4 teaspoon cayenne pepper
1 teaspoon dried basil
1/2 teaspoon dried oregano
Salt, pepper
Tomato slices and onion rings for serving

Directions:
1. Put the black beans into a blender or food processor and pulse a couple of times until a smooth paste forms. Transfer the beans into a bowl and add the onion and red bell pepper.
2. Put the walnuts and pumpkin seeds in a food processor together with the garlic and process until ground. Add them to the bowl with the rest of the ingredients. Stir in the wheat germ, nutritional yeast, basil, oregano, cayenne pepper and salt and pepper to taste. Mix well then wet your hands and form burgers.
3. Heat a grill pan and brush it with plenty of olive oil. Cook the formed burgers on both sides 6-7 minutes until cooked through and golden brown.

Simple Zucchini Burgers

One of the easiest but, at the same time, the tastiest burger recipes, these are made in a flash. All it takes is a good quality, fresh zucchini and some olive oil, flavored with a pinch of dried herbs.

Servings: 4-6 burgers

Ingredients:
1 zucchini, cut in 1/4 inch thick slices
2 tablespoons olive oil
1 tablespoon balsamic vinegar
Salt, pepper
Vegan burger buns
Tomato slices, lettuce leaves

Directions:
1. Put the zucchini slices in a colander and sprinkle a generous amount of salt. Let them sit there for 30 minutes. This is done to extract the natural bitterness of the zucchini. After 30 minutes, rinse well and drain on paper towels.
2. Transfer them into a bowl and drizzle the olive oil. Toss to evenly coat the slices.
3. Heat your grill or grill pan and cook the zucchini slices 3-4 minutes on each side, just to be tender. Remove them into a bowl and drizzle a bit of balsamic vinegar. Sprinkle some freshly ground pepper
4. Serve them layered on vegan burger buns with tomato slices, lettuce and basil leaves.

Sweet Potato Grilled Burgers

Although sweet potatoes have that slightly sweet taste, when combined with beans, they make a surprisingly delicious burger.

Servings: 8-10 burgers

Ingredients:
3 cups cannellini white beans, drained
2 sweet potatoes, peeled then boiled and mashed
3 tablespoons tahini paste
1 teaspoon Cajun seasoning
1/3 cup whole wheat flour
Salt, pepper to taste
Avocado slices, tomatoes, and onion rings for serving

Directions:
1. Put the beans in a food processor or blender and puree until smooth. Transfer the mixture into a bowl and stir in the mashed potatoes, followed by the tahini paste and Cajun seasoning. Add the whole wheat flour and a pinch of salt and pepper and mix well. Wet your hands and form small patties. Set aside.
2. Heat a grill pan and brush it with plenty of olive oil. Cook the burgers on the grill on both sides for 7-8 minutes until cooked through and browned.
3. Serve on vegan burger buns with avocado slices, tomato slices and onion rings.

Grilled Tofu and Portobello Burgers

Pairing tofu with mushrooms is a great idea, especially because the tofu has a very mild flavor and it will borrow flavor from the mushrooms, creating a delicious vegan burger.

Servings: 4 burgers

Ingredients:
4 Portobello mushrooms
1 large red onion, sliced
1 tablespoon balsamic vinegar
2 garlic cloves, minced
2 tablespoons olive oil
10 oz firm packed tofu
1/2 cup red wine
1 tablespoon soy sauce
1 teaspoon honey
1 tablespoon sesame seeds
Salt, pepper
Vegan burger buns
Tomato slices and arugula to garnish

Directions:
1. In a bowl, whisk together the red wine with soy sauce, honey, sesame seeds and a pinch of freshly ground pepper. Put the tofu, cut into slices, in this marinade and leave for 30 minutes to infuse the flavors.
2. Remove the stems from the mushrooms and sprinkle them with a pinch of salt and pepper. Heat a grill pan and cook the mushrooms on both sides until cooked through and browned on the surface.
3. Remove the tofu from the marinade and grill it in the same pan as the mushrooms, on both sides, until golden brown.
4. Mix the red onion with garlic, balsamic vinegar and olive oil.
5. Serve the mushrooms on vegan burger buns, topped with a slice of grilled tofu and some marinated red onion.

Pineapple and Mushroom Burgers

Having a Hawaiian taste, this burger is a real delight for the taste buds because of its sweet and smoky taste and crunchy texture.

Servings: 2 burgers

Ingredients:
2 Portobello mushrooms
2 slices fresh pineapple
1/4 cup teriyaki sauce
1 teaspoon honey
Salt, pepper
Vegan burger buns

Directions:
1. Mix the teriyaki sauce with the honey and a pinch of salt and freshly ground pepper, then brush the mushrooms and pineapple with this sauce.
2. Heat a grill pan on a medium flame and cook both the mushrooms and pineapple on both sides 6-7 minutes on both sides until golden brown and cooked through.
3. Layer the mushrooms and pineapple slices on a burger bun and serve warm.

Bulgur and Chickpeas Burgers

Bulgur is a very healthy whole grain and combined with chickpeas, it is delicious.

Servings: 6-8 burgers

Ingredients:
3 oz bulgur
2 cups water
1 1/2 cups canned chickpeas
1/2 cup fresh chopped parsley
1 tablespoon all purpose flour
2 garlic cloves, minced
2 tablespoons breadcrumbs
1 tablespoon olive oil
Salt, pepper

Directions:
1. Pour the water into a saucepan and bring to a boil. Throw in the bulgur and cook it until all the liquid has been absorbed. Set aside to cool down, then transfer it into a bowl.
2. Put the chickpeas in a food processor or blender and pulse a few times until a smooth paste forms. Transfer the paste into the bowl with the bulgur.
3. Stir in the chopped parsley, flour, breadcrumbs and garlic, and season with salt and pepper to taste.
4. Wet your hands and form small burgers.
5. Heat a grill pan on a medium flame and brush it with olive oil. Cook the burgers on both sides until golden brown. Serve it on vegan burger buns with tomato slices or guacamole dip.

Roasted Bell Pepper and Quinoa Burgers

Roasting bell peppers helps them develop a sweet and smoky flavor you will love. Mixed with quinoa, they make an excellent, delicious burger.

Servings: 6-8 burgers

Ingredients:
2/3 cup uncooked quinoa
3 cups water or vegetable broth
4 roasted red bell peppers
1 cup canned white beans
2 tablespoons chopped coriander
Salt, pepper

Directions:
1. Pour the water or stock into a pan and bring to a boil. Stir in the uncooked quinoa and set the pan aside until the quinoa absorbs all the liquid.
2. Put the bell pepper and white beans in a food processor and pulse a few times until a smooth paste forms. Transfer the paste into a bowl, then stir in the quinoa and chopped coriander. Season with freshly ground pepper and a touch of salt.
3. Wet your hands and form small burgers.
4. Heat a grill pan and brush it with a bit of vegetable oil. Cook the burgers on the grill on both sides for 6-7 minutes until golden brown and crusty.

Roasted Onion and Portobello Burgers

Roasting the onion only enhances its natural sweetness and adds a smoky aroma that we can only love, especially combined with other earthy flavors such as mushrooms.

Servings: 2 burgers

Ingredients:
1 large green onion, cut into rings
2 tablespoons olive oil
2 Portobello mushrooms
1 teaspoon balsamic vinegar
1/8 teaspoon chili flakes
1 teaspoon honey
1 teaspoon soy sauce
Salt, pepper
2 Vegan burger buns

Directions:
1. Heat the olive oil in a saucepan and stir in the onion. Sauté on low heat for 15-20 minutes until soft and slightly browned. Remove from heat and add the chili flakes and balsamic vinegar.
2. In another bowl, mix the soy sauce with honey and a pinch of freshly ground pepper. Brush the mushrooms with this mixture then grill them on a preheated grill pan until they are cooked through.
3. Cut the buns in half lengthwise then layer the mushrooms and onion mixture between the 2 parts of the bun. Serve right away.

Tropical Black Bean Burgers

The tropical flavors in these burgers are strong, but not overpowering. The end result is slightly sweet but savory and packed with lots of flavors that will make you think of summer and warm weather.

Servings: 6-8 burgers

Ingredients:
3 cups canned black beans, drained
1/2 cup rolled oats
4 tablespoons sweet corn
1/4 cup crushed pineapple
1 teaspoon mustard
Salt, pepper

Directions:
1. Rinse the black beans and put them in a food processor together with the rolled oats and pulse a few times until well blended and smooth. Transfer to a large bowl and stir in the sweet corn, pineapple and mustard. Season with freshly ground pepper and salt and form small patties with your wet or greased hands.
2. Heat a grill pan on a medium flame and brush it with plenty of vegetable oil. Cook the burgers on the grill for 6-7 minutes on each side until browned and crisp on the surface. Serve them warm.

Almond and Tofu Burgers

Combining the texture of tofu with the crunch of almonds and their earthy flavor, these burgers will surely be a delight for your taste buds and impress even those who still eat meat.

Servings: 6-8 burgers

Ingredients:
2 tablespoons flax seeds, freshly ground
4 tablespoons water
1 package firm tofu, crumbled
1 carrot, peeled and grated
2 green onions, finely chopped
2 tablespoons sesame oil
1 teaspoon grated ginger
2 garlic cloves, minced
2/3 cup slivered almonds, toasted
2 teaspoons soy sauce
1 tablespoon sesame seeds
Vegan burger buns
Tomato slices

Directions:
1. In a small bowl, mix the flax seeds with water and set aside.
2. Heat the sesame oil in a heavy skillet. Add the green onion, carrot, garlic and ginger, and sauté for 4-5 minutes on low heat until they are soft. Transfer into a bowl and stir in the crumbled tofu, flax seed mixture, almonds, soy sauce and sesame seeds. Mix well to combine then form small patties.
3. Heat a grill pan over a medium flame and cook the burgers on each side for 5-6 minutes.
4. Serve on vegan burger buns with tomato slices or your favorite toppings.

Broccoli and Mushroom Grilled Burgers

With its mild flavor, broccoli tastes great combined with other ingredients and spiced with garlic and other aromatic herbs or condiments.

Servings: 6-8 burgers

Ingredients:
1 small red onion, finely chopped
2 garlic cloves, minced
2 tablespoons olive oil
2 cups chopped mushrooms
1 cup cooked quinoa
1 1/2 cup canned pinto beans
2 carrots, peeled and sliced
1/2 head of broccoli, cut into florets
1/2 teaspoon cumin seeds
Salt, pepper
2 tablespoons chopped coriander leaves

Directions:
1. Heat the oil in a heavy skillet and stir in the onion and garlic. Sauté for 2 minutes then add the chopped mushrooms and keep cooking until they are soft and all the liquid has evaporated.
2. Put the carrots and broccoli florets into a steamer and cook them for 10 minutes until soft. Put them in a bowl and coarsely mash them. Stir in the sautéed onion and garlic. Mix in the mashed beans and quinoa, followed by the cumin seeds and a pinch of salt and pepper. Mix well until the mixture comes together.
3. Wet your hands and form patties. Set them aside.
4. Heat a grill pan over a medium flame. Brush it with a small amount of olive oil then cook the burgers on each side for 4-5 minutes until they form a golden brown crust.
5. Serve them on vegan burger buns with tomato slices, lettuce leaves, mustard, or any other topping you like.

Sweet Corn and Sweet Potato Burgers

If you are not used to the taste of sweet potatoes, you might find this burger rather sweet, but give it a go anyway. It's flavorful and very healthy.

Servings: 8-10 burgers

Ingredients:
2 pounds sweet potatoes, peeled and cubed
2 tablespoons olive oil
1 onion, finely chopped
1 green chili, chopped
1 teaspoon dried coriander
2 cups canned sweet corn
1 cup cornmeal
2 tablespoons packed parsley leaves, chopped
Salt, pepper
Vegan burger buns, onion, lettuce, tomatoes

Directions:
1. Put the potatoes in a deep dish baking pan, season with salt and pepper, drizzle with a bit of olive oil and cover the pan with foil. Cook in a preheated oven at 375º F until they are tender.
2. Remove from oven, transfer to a bowl and mash well with a fork. Stir in the onion, chili, coriander and parsley, the sweet corn and the cornmeal. Adjust the taste with salt and pepper and form small patties with your wet hands.
3. Heat a grill pan over a medium flame and brush it with vegetable oil. Grill the burgers on each side for 6-7 minutes until crusty and browned.
4. Serve on vegan burger buns topped with onion rings, lettuce leaves and tomatoes.

Spicy Thai Vegan Burger

Spicy and flavorful, this burger is great for lunch as a takeaway meal. It is healthy and fairly easy to make, but has all those Thai flavors that will surely impress the audience.

Servings: 10-12 burgers

Ingredients:

4 cups canned white beans
1 cup rolled oats
1 teaspoon cumin
1 teaspoon fresh ginger, grated
2 garlic cloves, minced
1 teaspoon turmeric
1 carrot, peeled and grated
1 cup fresh pea pods
4 cherry tomatoes, quartered
2 green onions, chopped
2 tablespoons fresh Thai basil, chopped
1/4 cup unsweetened coconut milk
1 teaspoon lime juice
1 red pepper, deseeded and sliced
Vegan burger buns
2 tablespoons vegetable oil
Salt, pepper

Directions:
1. Put the beans, garlic, ginger and turmeric into a food processor and pulse until a paste forms. Transfer into a bowl and stir in the rolled oats. Let it rest 30 minutes then wet your hands and form small patties.
2. Heat a grill pan on medium flame, brush it with vegetable oil and grill the burgers on each side for 6-7 minutes or until crusty and browned
3. To make the vegetable garnish, thinly slice the pea pods and put them in a bowl together with the carrots, tomatoes, chopped basil and green onions.
4. In another bowl, whisk together the coconut milk, lime juice and red pepper and pour the mixture over the vegetables in the bowl. Mix to evenly coat them.
5. Serve the burgers on buns with a spoon of vegetable mix.

Yellow Squash Burgers

Yellow squash is similar to zucchini in both shape and taste and it is a great choice for vegans. Combine it with other tasty ingredients to create a delicious, flavorful burger.

Servings: 6-8

Ingredients':
1 yellow squash, chopped
1 zucchini, chopped
1 1/2 cups cooked brown rice
1 cup breadcrumbs
3 tablespoons tomato puree
1 tablespoon flax seeds, ground
3 tablespoons water
Salt, pepper
Vegetable oil

Directions:
1. It is very easy to make. First, mix the ground flax seeds with water and set aside. Mix the other ingredients together in another bowl then stir in the soaked flax seeds. Mix to combine well, add a bit of salt and pepper and then form small patties.
2. Heat a grill pan and brush it with vegetable oil. Grill the burgers on each side for 6-7 minutes or until crusty and browned on the outside but juicy on the inside.
3. Serve on vegan burger buns with your favorite topping.

Buckwheat and Grilled Pineapple Burgers

Despite its name, buckwheat is not a grain, but a fruit, being part of the same family as rhubarb. No matter its origins, it is very healthy and nutritious and it has a lovely texture after cooking.

Servings: 6-8 burgers

Ingredients:
2 1/2 cup canned beans, drained and rinsed
1/2 cup buckwheat
1 onion, chopped
2 garlic cloves
1/2 teaspoon chili powder
1 teaspoon cumin
1 teaspoon dried oregano
2 tablespoons olive oil
1 fresh pineapple, cut into thin slices
Salt, pepper

Directions:
1. Pour 1 1/5 cups water into a pan and bring to a boil. Add the buckwheat and cook on low to medium heat for 10-15 minutes or until all the liquid has been absorbed. Set aside.
2. Put the beans in a food processor together with the garlic, chili, cumin, oregano and olive oil. Pulse a few times until they transform into a paste then stir in the buckwheat and a pinch of salt and pepper. Mix well (not blend) and form small patties.
3. Heat the grill or grill pan and cook the burgers on each side for 5-6 minutes. When the burgers are done, grill the pineapple slices as well.
4. Serve the patties and pineapple layered on vegan burger buns.

Leek and Broccoli Burgers

Similar to onions in flavor, leeks are a bit milder but just as flavorful and versatile. These burgers are easy to make and they can be a great way to make your kids eat their green veggies as well.

Servings: 4-6 burgers

Ingredients:
1 head broccoli, trimmed and cut into florets
2 leeks, finely chopped (only the white part)
1 tablespoon flax seeds, ground
2 tablespoons water
2 potatoes, peeled and cubed
3 tablespoons olive oil
1 teaspoon dried thyme
Salt, pepper

Directions:
1. Mix the flax seeds with the water in a bowl and let them soak. This will substitute the egg.
2. Put the broccoli florets and potato cubes in a steamer and cook for 15-20 minutes until tender. Transfer into a bowl and mash them together with a fork.
3. Heat the olive oil in a large pan and sauté the leeks for 5-6 minutes until soft.
4. Combine the mashed broccoli mixture with the flax seeds and leeks then adjust the taste with salt and pepper.
5. Form small patties and grill them in a grill pan on each side for 5-6 minutes until just slightly browned.

Soybean and Pecan Burgers

One of the easiest ways to include soy in your vegan diet is through burgers. This particular recipe combines the soybeans with pecans for a boost of fiber and nutrients.

Servings: 6-8 burgers

Ingredients:
3 cups canned soybeans, drained
1/2 cup sunflower seeds
1/2 cup pecans
1/2 teaspoon cayenne pepper
1 carrot, peeled and grated
2 garlic cloves, minced
1 celery stalk, finely chopped
2 cups rolled oats
Salt, pepper

Directions:
1. Take the bowl of a food processor and combine the soybeans, sunflower seeds, pecans, cayenne pepper and a pinch of salt. Pulse a few times until smooth then transfer into a bowl.
2. Stir in the carrot, garlic and celery, then the rolled oats. Taste and add more salt if needed. Wet or grease your hands and form small patties. Cook them all on the grill pan, on each side, for 5-6 minutes or until crusty and browned.
3. Serve them on vegan burger buns with your favorite toppings.

Tofu and Onion Marmalade Burgers

By cooking the onion into a marmalade, we remove its tanginess but we add more flavors and sweetness so it goes well with the grilled, marinated tofu.

Servings: 2 burgers

Ingredients:
2 tofu slices
1 tablespoon soy sauce
1 tablespoon honey
1 tablespoon lemon juice
3 red onions, sliced
1/4 cup red wine
2 tablespoons rice vinegar
5 tablespoons brown sugar
1 star anise
Salt, pepper

Directions:
1. In a bowl, mix the soy sauce, honey and lemon juice. Add the tofu slices and toss to evenly coat them. Heat your grill or grill pan and cook the tofu on each side for 4-5 minutes until slightly browned.
2. In another pan, combine the onions, brown sugar, red wine and vinegar, plus star anise. Put the pan on medium to low flame and bring to a boil then simmer for 15-20 minutes until soft and fragrant.
3. Serve the tofu slices on vegan burger buns with a dollop of marmalade.

Spinach and Pistachio Burgers

One great way to make your kids eat their green veggies is to hide them in burgers. This particular recipe combines the nutrients of the spinach with the fiber and aroma of the pistachio, creating a delicious, moist burger.

Servings: 6-8 burgers

Ingredients:
3 cups spinach leaves
1 green onion, chopped
2 cups canned white beans
2/3 cup pistachio, ground
1 cup rolled oats
1 teaspoon cumin
1 teaspoon soy sauce
Salt, pepper

Directions:
1. Put the spinach in a steamer and cook for 2 minutes. Remove and chop finely then transfer into a bowl.
2. Put the beans in a food processor and pulse a few times until a paste forms. Add it to the bowl as well. Stir in the green onion, ground pistachio, rolled oats, cumin and soy sauce. Adjust the taste with salt and pepper and form small burgers.
3. Heat a grill or grill pan on a medium flame and cook the burgers on both sides for 5-6 minutes or until browned and crusty.
4. Serve on vegan burger buns, simply or with your favorite toppings.

Chapter 2: Fried Burgers

Vegan burgers are easy to make and include only healthy, top quality ingredients. They can be cooked in different ways, each having its own advantages and disadvantages.

This chapter includes a variety of fried burgers. Do not be afraid of the word "fried". It doesn't mean they are cooked in a bath of oil; therefore, they are not harmful for your health in any way. They are simply coated in flour or different seeds and fried in vegetable oil until a golden crust is formed. The big advantage of frying them is their taste. Vegetables take on a different flavor when fried in hot oil rather than grilled or baked. Plus, not many people have a grill or the time to turn their oven on to bake their food. Frying is, after all, available for everyone and it's easy to do.

Pinto Burgers with Chipotle Aioli

Pinto beans are very common and easy to find. Therefore, making this burger won't be a hassle as all the ingredients are on hand, but very delicious combined together. Served with the spicy aioli, it becomes a meal that will surely awaken your senses.

Servings: 6-8 burgers

Ingredients:

For burgers:
2 cups canned pinto beans, drained and rinsed
1 red onion, finely chopped
1 red pepper, finely chopped
1/2 cup sweet corn, fresh or frozen
2 tablespoons vegetable oil
2 garlic cloves, minced
1 teaspoon cumin powder
1/2 teaspoon dried oregano
2 tablespoons tomato puree
Salt, pepper
1/4 cup cornmeal
Oil for frying

For the chipotle aioli:
1/2 cup coconut yogurt
1 chipotle in adobo sauce, finely chopped
1 tablespoon adobo sauce
1 garlic clove, minced
1 pinch of salt

Directions:

To make the burgers:
1. Put the beans in a bowl and, using a potato masher, coarsely mash them. Set aside.
2. Heat the olive oil in a medium pan and sauté the onion until translucent. Stir in the garlic, pepper and corn, and cook 5 more minutes. Transfer this mixture into the bowl with the beans. Stir in the cumin, dried oregano, tomato purée , cornmeal and a pinch of salt and freshly ground pepper. Mix well then wet your hands and form small patties.
3. Heat a small quantity of oil in a frying pan and cook each burger on both sides for 5-6 minutes or until crusty and golden brown

To make the aioli:
1. Mix the coconut yogurt with the chopped chipotle, adobo sauce, garlic and a pinch of salt.
2. Serve the burgers on buns with a lettuce leaf and a dollop of aioli sauce.

Fennel and Beetroot Burger

Having a strong flavor, fennel is not liked by everyone but combined with the mild beetroot, its flavor tones down, creating a delicious burger for you to enjoy.

Servings: 6-8 burgers

Ingredients:
2 medium size beetroots, peeled and grated
2 tablespoons chopped dill
1 fennel bulb, trimmed and finely chopped
1 cup cooked brown rice
2 tablespoons cornmeal
1/4 cup tomato sauce
Salt, pepper
Vegetable oil for frying

Directions:
1. In a large bowl, mix together the grated beets, fennel, dill, brown rice and cornmeal. Stir in the tomato sauce and a pinch of salt and pepper then form small patties.
2. Heat a small quantity of vegetable oil in a large skillet and fry the burgers on each side for 6-7 minutes. They should be crusty and golden brown.
3. Serve on vegan burger buns with your favorite toppings

Curried Mushroom Burgers

Mushrooms and curry pair wonderfully together, enhancing each other's taste. This particular burger is delicate with a strong earthy flavor, and has the advantage of being able to be paired with any toppings.

Servings: 6-8 burgers

Ingredients:
2 cups mushrooms, finely chopped
1 onion, chopped
2 garlic cloves, minced
1 teaspoon curry powder
1 cup canned chickpeas, drained
2 carrots, peeled and grated
3 oz walnuts, chopped
2 tablespoons chopped coriander
2 tablespoons flour
Salt, pepper
Oil for frying

Directions:
1. Heat 1 tablespoon olive oil in a frying pan and sauté the onion and garlic for 2 minutes. Stir in curry, followed by the carrots and mushrooms. Cook for 10 minutes on low heat. Set aside.
2. Put the chickpeas in a food processor and pulse a few times until a smooth paste forms. Transfer into a bowl and add the mushroom mixture. Stir in the walnuts, coriander and flour, then adjust the taste with salt and pepper. Wet your hands and form small burgers. Put them aside on a cutting board or parchment paper.
3. Heat a small amount of vegetable oil in a large frying pan and cook the burgers on each side for 6-7 minutes or until crusty and golden brown. Serve on vegan burger buns with your favorite toppings.

Chickpea and Sweet Corn B

Nutritious and filling, these burgers will become a perso
of their lovely, but mild, flavor and juicy insides.

Servings: 6-8 burgers

Ingredients:
1 1/3 cups fresh or frozen sweet corn
1 1/2 cup canned chickpeas, drained and rinsed
2 tablespoons flax seeds, ground
6 tablespoons water
1/4 cup cornmeal
1/2 cup all purpose whole wheat flour
1 teaspoon baking powder
1/4 cup chopped green onions
Salt, pepper

Directions:
1. In a small bowl, whisk together the ground flax seeds with water and set aside 10 minutes
2. Put the chickpeas in a blender and pulse until a smooth paste forms. Transfer into a bowl and mix in the flax seeds, corn, cornmeal, flour and baking powder, as well as chopped green onions. Give it a good mix to combine well then wet your hands and form small patties. Set them aside.
3. Heat a small quantity of vegetable oil in a pan and fry the burgers on each side for 5-6 minutes until golden brown.
4. Serve on vegan burger buns with your favorite toppings (tomato slices, lettuce leaves, shredded cabbage, etc.).

Fried Potato and Garlic Burgers

Potato patties are so delicious that they will surely become a favorite. Plus, they can be made ahead of time and simply served to your family for lunch or dinner

Servings: 6-8 burgers

Ingredients:
2 pounds potatoes, peeled and cubed
3 garlic cloves, minced
1/2 cup flour, plus more for coating
2 tablespoons fresh chopped dill
salt, pepper
1/4 cup vegetable oil

Directions:
1. Pour a few cups of water in a large pot and add a pinch of salt. Throw in the potato cubes and boil until they are tender. Remove from water and mash the potatoes until smooth.
2. Stir in the garlic cloves and dill and adjust the taste with freshly ground pepper and salt. Mix in the flour then form burgers with your wet hands. Set them aside.
3. Heat the oil in a large heavy skillet and fry the burgers on both sides 4-5 minutes or until they are golden brown.
4. Serve them on vegan burger buns with a vegan yogurt and dill sauce.

Broccoli and Pistachio Spicy Burgers

Not everyone likes broccoli, but you won't even notice them in these burgers. The flavor that shines through is the pistachio, together with the heat of the chili.

Servings: 4-6 burgers

Ingredients:
1/3 cup pistachio, shelled and slightly toasted
3 cups broccoli florets
1/4 teaspoon chili flakes
1/3 cup rolled oats
2 tablespoons pumpkin seeds
2 tablespoons sunflower seeds
2 tablespoons black sesame
Salt, pepper
Oil for Frying

Directions:
1. Put the broccoli florets in a steamer and cook them until tender. Transfer them into a food processor together with the pistachio and chili flakes. Pulse a few times until the mixture sticks together.
2. Put the broccoli mixture into a large bowl then stir in the rolled oats and seeds. Adjust the taste with salt and pepper and form small patties with your wet hands.
3. Put a few tablespoons of olive oil in a frying pan or heavy skillet and cook the burgers in the hot oil, on medium flame, on both sides, until golden brown and crusty.
4. Serve them on vegan burger buns with tomato slices and lettuce leaves.

Beet and Quinoa Black Bean Burgers

Although beet is not the most consumed vegetable, keep in mind that it is delicious and it works great paired with other vegetables.

Servings: 6-8 burgers

Ingredients:
1 small onion, finely chopped
1 tablespoon olive oil
1 medium size beet, peeled and grated
2 cups baby spinach leaves
1 1/2 cup canned black beans, drained and rinsed
1 1/2 cup cooked quinoa
1/4 cup rolled oats
1 teaspoon sugar
1 teaspoon chopped rosemary
Salt, pepper
Oil for frying

Directions:
1. Heat the olive oil in a heavy skillet and add the onion. Sauté for 4 minutes then stir in the spinach and beet and cook for 5 more minutes. Set aside to cool then transfer into a bowl.
2. Put the black beans in a food processor and puree them until smooth. Put the paste over the beet in the bowl. Stir in the rolled oats, quinoa, sugar and rosemary. Adjust the taste with salt and pepper then form small patties with your wet hands as the mixture tends to be sticky.
3. Pour a few tablespoons of oil in a frying pan then cook the burgers in the hot oil on both sides until golden brown and crusty.
4. Serve them warm on vegan burger buns with onion rings and tomato slices.

Chipotle Black Bean Burgers

This burger is one of those foods you think you wouldn't like at first, but then have the surprise of your life after tasting it. They are spicy but the heat is not overwhelming, yet all the flavors shine through.

Servings: 8-10 burgers

Ingredients:
3 cups canned black beans
1 small onion, finely chopped
2 garlic cloves
2 tablespoons chipotle in adobo
1 teaspoon cumin powder
2 tablespoons cornstarch
2 tablespoons chopped coriander
1/2 cups rolled oats
4 tablespoons olive oil
Salt, pepper

Directions:
1. Put the onion, garlic and black beans in a food processor or blender and pulse a few times until well combined and purée d. Add chipotle, cumin powder, coriander, cornstarch and a pinch of salt. Pulse a few more times to combine then transfer the mixture to a large bowl. Mix in the rolled oats then form the burgers with your wet hands.
2. Heat the olive oil in a large, heavy skillet over a medium flame then cook the burgers in the hot oil on both sides until golden brown and crisp at the edges.
3. Serve immediately on vegan burger buns with your favorite toppings.

Carrot and Parsnip Burgers

Carrot and parsnip are pretty common ingredients in everyone's pantry but they are delicious and very fragrant paired together in any dish, especially in these burgers considering they are the only main ingredients.

Servings: 4-6 burgers

Ingredients:
2 carrots, peeled and grated
1 parsnip, peeled and grated
1 1/2 cups cooked quinoa
1 cup canned white beans
2 tablespoons rice flour
Salt, pepper

Directions:
1. Put the white beans in a food processor and pulse a few times until a paste forms. Transfer the paste into a large bowl then stir in the grated carrot, parsnip, cooked quinoa and rice flour. Season with freshly ground pepper and a pinch of salt. Form burgers with your wet hands and set them aside.
2. Heat a small amount of olive oil in a large frying pan then cook the burgers on both sides, until golden brown, or about 6-7 minutes.
3. Serve them on vegan burger buns with your favorite toppings.

Curry and Chickpea Burgers

Full of extraordinary flavors, these burgers are delicious, creamy and easy to make.

Servings: 6-8 burgers

Ingredients:
1/4 cup rolled oats
3 cups canned chickpeas, drained
2 garlic cloves
1 teaspoon curry powder
2 tablespoons chopped coriander
3 tablespoons olive oil
Salt, pepper

Directions:
1. Combine the rolled oats and chickpeas in a food processor. Process them until smooth. Add the garlic cloves, curry and coriander. Pulse a few more times then transfer into a bowl. Adjust the taste with salt and pepper then form burgers with your wet hands.
2. Heat a large frying pan and add some olive oil. Fry the burgers on both sides for 5-6 minutes until golden brown and crusty. Remove them onto paper towels and serve them on vegan burger buns with cucumber and tomato slices.

Curried Vegetable Burgers

Vegetables combined with curry are a delight for your taste buds. A bit spicy but flavorful, these burgers can easily replace any meal of the day and are filling and nutritious.

Servings: 8-10 burgers

Ingredients:
1 3/4 cups canned chickpeas, drained
2 1/2 cups canned lentils, drained
1/2 cup cashew nuts
2 carrots, peeled and grated
3 garlic cloves, minced
1 green onion, chopped
2 tablespoon olive oil
1 teaspoon curry powder
1 teaspoon turmeric powder
4 tablespoons flour
2 cups breadcrumbs
3 tablespoons olive oil
Salt, pepper

Directions:
1. Heat the olive oil in a heavy skillet and add the onion and garlic. Sauté for a few minutes until soft and translucent then stir in the carrots and keep cooking until soft. Transfer the mixture into a bowl then mix in the lentils, curry powder, and turmeric.
2. Put the chickpeas and cashew nuts in a food processor and pulse a few times until a smooth paste form. Stir this paste into the vegetable mix then add the flour. Season with a pinch of salt and freshly ground pepper then wet your hands and form burgers. Coat each burger with breadcrumbs and set them aside.
3. Heat 3 tablespoons vegetable oil in a large frying pan and cook the burgers for 5-6 minutes on both sides until golden brown and crusty
4. Serve on Vegan burger buns with your favorite toppings.

Spicy Quinoa Burgers

Quinoa is a super food, healthy and packed with lots of nutrients and fibers. It works great in burgers because of its mild flavor, which allows the rest of the ingredients to be the stars.

Servings: 6-8 burgers

Ingredients:
1 small onion, chopped
1 green pepper, deseeded and chopped
2 garlic cloves, minced
1 cup canned black beans
1 cup cooked quinoa
1 teaspoon taco seasoning
2 tablespoons flax seeds
1/2 cup breadcrumbs
2 tablespoons all purpose flour
Salt, pepper
Oil for frying

Directions:
1. In a small bowl, mix together the flax seeds with 6 tablespoons water and let them soak.
2. Heat a small amount of vegetable oil in a heavy skillet and add the onion and garlic. Cook for 4 minutes until soft, then transfer into a bowl.
3. Put half of the quinoa and the black beans in a food processor or blender. Pulse a few times until well blended and smooth. Add to the bowl and stir in the remaining quinoa, taco seasoning and green pepper. Give it a good mix then add the flour, breadcrumbs and soaked flax seeds. Wet your hands and form burgers.
4. In a frying pan, heat a small amount of vegetable oil and fry the burgers on both sides for 5-6 minutes until golden brown and crisp.

Zucchini Fried Burgers

From soups to stews, zucchini are delicious and easy to prepare. In this recipe, they team with tomatoes to create an amazingly delicious vegan burger than will impress even meat lovers.

Servings: 6-8 burgers

Ingredients:
4 oz bread, cubed
2 tablespoons flax seeds
1 red bell pepper, cored and chopped
1 zucchini, grated
2 tablespoons chives, chopped
1 garlic clove, minced
3 tablespoons flour
Salt, pepper

Directions:
1. Mix the flax seeds with 2 tablespoons of water and let them soak.
2. Put the bread in a bowl and cover it with water. Let it soak a few minutes then squeeze off the liquid. Stir in the flax seeds and grated zucchini, then the diced bell pepper, garlic and flour. Adjust the taste with salt and pepper and form burgers with your wet hands.
3. Heat some vegetable oil in a frying pan or skillet and cook the burgers on both sides until golden brown.
4. Serve them on vegan burger buns or baguettes with tomato slices, onion rings and lettuce leaves.

Peanut Butter Chickpea Burgers

Although it may sound like a weird combination, peanut butter's earthy flavor balances up perfectly with the chickpeas and the rest of the spices.

Servings: 6-8 burgers

Ingredients:
2 cups canned chickpeas
3 tablespoons peanut butter
1 teaspoon lemon juice
1 teaspoon soy sauce
1 teaspoon fresh grated ginger
1 green onion, chopped
1/4 teaspoon chili flakes
3 tablespoons coconut oil
Salt, pepper if needed

Directions:
1. Drain the chickpeas then put them in a food processor or blender and pulse a few times to ground them. Add the peanut butter, soy sauce, lemon juice and ginger, and pulse until well combined. Transfer into a bowl and stir in the green onion, chili flakes, and a pinch of salt and pepper if needed.
2. Wet or grease your hands and form burgers. Heat the coconut oil in a pan and fry the burgers on both sides until browned and crusty.

Eggplant and Cumin Burgers

Eggplants are great for making burgers because of their texture, not to mention, their unique taste when combined with other ingredients, such as garlic and cumin.

Servings: 4-6 burgers

Ingredients:
2 large eggplant
1 red onion, finely chopped
2 garlic cloves
1 cup breadcrumbs
1 teaspoon cumin seeds
1 tablespoon chopped parsley
1 teaspoon chopped fresh mint
Salt, pepper

Directions:
1. Cut the eggplant in half, sprinkle some salt and pepper and put the halves in a pan. Cook the eggplant in the oven at 240C for 30-40 minutes until soft. Remove from oven and let them cool, then scoop the flesh into a bowl. Stir in the garlic, cumin seeds, parsley, mint, onion and breadcrumbs. Season with a pinch of salt and pepper and refrigerate the mixture for 1 hour.
2. Wet your hands and form small patties.
3. Pour a few tablespoons of oil in a large pan and heat it up. Cook the burgers in the oil for 6-7 minutes on each side or until just golden brown and cooked through.
4. Serve on vegan burger buns with tomato and avocado slices and a dollop of coconut yogurt

Garlic Potato Burgers

Although very common ingredients, potatoes are also the most versatile ones. Their flavor works well with anything else, especially with garlic.

Servings: 8-10 burgers

Ingredients:
8 oz potatoes, grated
3 garlic cloves, minced
1 teaspoon dried thyme
1 teaspoon paprika
1/2 cup breadcrumbs
3/4 cup all purpose flour
2 tablespoons olive oil
2 tablespoons flax seeds, ground
4 tablespoons water
Oil for frying

Directions:
1. In a small bowl, whisk the flax seeds with water and set them aside.
2. Put the potatoes, garlic, thyme and paprika in a bowl and mix well. Stir in the oil, breadcrumbs and flour, then the flax seeds, and mix well to combine. Grease your hands and form small burgers. Set them aside.
3. Heat a small quantity of vegetable oil in a frying pan and cook the burgers on each side for 5-7 minutes, flipping them over to evenly cook them.
4. Serve the burgers on buns with your favorite toppings

Eggplant and Cauliflower Fried Burgers

Tangy, smoky and rich, these burgers are a delight for your senses, packing lots of flavors and aromas.

Servings: 6-8 burgers

Ingredients:
1 eggplant
1 head cauliflower, cut into florets
1/2 cup rolled oats
2 tablespoons cornmeal
1 teaspoon dried basil
1 teaspoon dried oregano
Salt, pepper
1/4 cup flour
Oil for frying

Directions:
1. Cut the eggplant in half lengthwise and put it on a baking tray. Bake in the oven at 350º F for 30-40 minutes until soft. Scoop out the flesh into a bowl and mash it with a fork.
2. Put the cauliflower florets in a steamer and cook them for 10-15 minutes until tender. Coarsely chop them and stir them in the bowl with the eggplant. Add the rolled oats, cornmeal, basil and oregano. Adjust the taste with salt and pepper. Form small burgers and coat each of them with flour. Set them aside.
3. Pour a few tablespoons of oil in a pan over a medium flame and cook the burgers on each side for 5-7 minutes until crisp and golden brown.
4. Serve them on vegan burger buns with your favorite toppings.

Okra Burgers

Okra is high in fiber and vitamin C so as a vegan, you should include it in your diet as it is also a very versatile vegetable.

Servings: 4-6 burgers

Ingredients:
1 pound okra, finely sliced
1 onion, chopped
1/2 cup cornmeal
2/3 cup all purpose flour
1/4 teaspoon baking powder
1/2 cup water
Salt, pepper
1 tablespoon flax seeds, ground
2 tablespoons water

Directions:
1. In a small bowl, whisk together the flax seeds with water and set aside.
2. Put the okra slices in a bowl, add the onion, cornmeal, flour, baking powder and water then stir in the flax seeds. Mix well, adding a touch of salt and pepper.
3. Take a large frying pan and heat a few tablespoons of oil. Drop spoonfuls of batter into the hot oil and fry them on each side for 3-4 minutes. Remove them onto paper towels.
4. Serve them on vegan burger buns with tomato slices, cucumber and onion rings.

Walnut and Brown Rice Vegan Burgers

Packed with good fats, these burgers are easy to make and you will be surprised at how good they actually taste.

Servings: 8-10 burgers

Ingredients:
2 1/2 cups cooked brown rice
1 small onion, finely chopped
1 small carrot, peeled and grated
3 garlic cloves, minced
2 cups walnuts, toasted and ground
1 teaspoon sesame seeds
3 tablespoons vegetable oil for frying
Salt, pepper
Vegan burger buns
Tomato slices for serving
Lettuce

Directions:
1. Mix the cooked rice with the carrot and garlic in a bowl. Add the onion then the ground walnuts. Mix until well blended. If the mixture doesn't stick together, add a bit of water. Stir in the sesame seeds and season with a pinch of salt and pepper.
2. Wet your hands and form small burgers. Set them aside.
3. Heat a large frying pan over a medium to high heat and add a few tablespoons of vegetable oil. Fry the burgers in the hot oil for 5-6 minutes on each side or until cooked through and golden brown on the surface.
4. Serve on vegan burger buns with tomato slices and lettuce leaves or cabbage salad.

Black Bean Burgers with Lime Dressing

Black beans are some of the most common ingredients when it comes to burgers, but they are delicious and make a very creamy burger. They also have a mild taste, which allows us to combine them with any other ingredients we wish.

Servings: 10-12 burgers

Ingredients:

2 red onions, chopped
1 carrot, peeled and grated
2 tablespoons olive oil
1 cup mushrooms, chopped
1 cup canned sweet corn, drained and rinsed
1 teaspoon cumin seeds
3 cups canned black beans, drained and rinsed
1 chipotle pepper, deseeded and chopped
1/2 cup cornmeal
1/2 cup breadcrumbs
Salt, pepper

For the lime dressing:
1/2 cup sour cream
Zest and juice from 1/2 lime
1/8 teaspoon cayenne pepper
Salt to taste

Directions:
1. Pour the olive oil into a heavy skillet and heat it. Stir in the onion and carrot and cook until they start to soften. Add the mushrooms, corn, pepper and cumin seeds and cook 10 more minutes, stirring frequently. Remove from heat and set aside.
2. Put the beans in a blender and mash them until fine. Transfer into a bowl and stir in the cooked mixture and cornmeal. Adjust the taste with salt and pepper and form burgers. It is best if you wet or grease your hands to prevent them from sticking. After each burger has been made, roll all of them through breadcrumbs.
3. Heat a small amount of vegetable oil in a frying pan and fry each burger on both sides, until golden brown and crusty.
4. To make the dressing, simply mix all the ingredients in a bowl.
5. Serve them on vegan burger buns with lime dressing and a lettuce leaf if you desire.

Beet and Black Bean Fried Burger

Beets are extremely healthy and you should include them in your vegan diet. They are delicious cooked in any way, from soups to stews, but they also make a great burger, combined with black beans.

Servings: 6-8 burgers

Ingredients:
1 cup cooked brown rice
1 small onion, finely chopped
2 large beets, peeled and grated
3 garlic cloves, minced
2 teaspoons cider vinegar
1 1/2 cups canned black beans, drained and rinsed
2 tablespoons olive oil
2 tablespoons chopped coriander leaves
2 tablespoons all purpose flour

Directions:
1. Heat the oil in a small, heavy skillet and sauté the onion until translucent and soft. Add the garlic and cook 1 more minute. Mix in the grated beets, lower the heat and cover the skillet with a lid. Cook 10-15 minutes, stirring occasionally, until they are soft. Stir in the vinegar and remove from heat.
2. Put the black beans in a bowl and purée them with a potato masher. Stir in the cooked beets, coriander leaves and rice. Stir in the flour and adjust the taste with a pinch of salt and pepper.
3. Wet or grease your hands and form small burgers. Set them aside.
4. Put a large frying pan over a medium flame and add a few tablespoons vegetable oil. Fry the burgers on each side for 5-6 minutes or until they form a golden brown crust. Serve them on vegan burger buns with your favorite toppings.

Cauliflower and Green Pea Burgers

Highly nutritious, these burgers are very healthy, containing just a few ingredients, but good ones, with vitamins and fiber.

Servings: 6-8 burgers

Ingredients:
1 head cauliflower, trimmed and cut into florets
1 cup green peas, frozen
1 teaspoon cumin
1 tablespoons fresh chopped mint
2 tablespoons fresh chopped coriander
1/2 cup cooked quinoa
2 tablespoons whole wheat flower
1 tablespoon flax seeds, ground
2 tablespoons water
Salt, pepper
Oil for frying

Directions:
1. In a small bowl, whisk the flax seeds with the water and set aside.
2. Put the cauliflower and green peas in a steamer and cook them 15-20 minutes or until just tender. Transfer into a bowl and mash them coarsely with a fork. Stir in the flax seeds, cumin, chopped herbs, quinoa and flour. Mix well until it comes together then form small burgers and set them aside.
3. Heat a small amount of vegetable oil in a large frying pan and cook the burgers on each side for 5-6 minutes, or until crusty and browned on the outside but moist on the inside.
4. Serve them on vegan burger buns with your favorite toppings.

Cilantro Bean Burgers with Spicy Guacamole

Cilantro is, in fact, a type of coriander and it holds the same intense aroma. It is delicious combined with beans and a spicy, creamy guacamole.

Servings: 8-10 burgers

Ingredients:

3/4 cup cooked quinoa
2 tablespoons olive oil
1 small red onion, finely chopped
2 garlic cloves, minced
2 tablespoons olive oil
2 cups canned pinto beans, drained
1 teaspoon smoked paprika
1/2 cup chopped cilantro
1/2 cup cornmeal
Salt, pepper

Lettuce leaves and tomato slices for serving
Vegan burger buns

For the spicy guacamole:
1 ripe avocado, peeled
1 teaspoon lemon juice
1/2 teaspoon cayenne pepper
1 tomato, peeled, deseeded, and diced
1 red onion, finely chopped
2 tablespoons coconut cream

Directions:

Heat the olive oil in a frying pan. Stir in the onion and garlic and cook 2-3 minutes. Add the beans and paprika and sauté for 2 minutes then remove from heat and purée the beans with a potato masher.

1. Put the purée in a bowl and stir in the cooked quinoa, cilantro, half of the cornmeal and a pinch of salt and freshly ground pepper.
2. Wet your hands and form small burgers. Coat each of them in the remaining cornmeal and set them aside.
3. Heat a small amount of vegetable oil in a frying pan and cook the burgers for 3-4 minutes on each side. The cornmeal will make a crunchy crust. Remove from oil onto paper towels and set aside.
4. To make the guacamole, put the avocado flesh in a bowl with the lemon juice and mash it with a fork. Stir in the cayenne pepper, coconut cream, tomato and red onion. Mix well to combine.
5. Serve the burgers on buns with a dollop of spicy guacamole

Pumpkin and Cumin Flavored Burgers

Pumpkin packs up an intense autumn flavor and is great both in sweet and savory dishes. This particular burger has an intense flavor and it's creamy, spicy and absolutely delicious.

Servings: 6-8 burgers

Ingredients:
1/4 cup olive oil
1 small red onion, finely chopped
1 red bell pepper, cored and chopped
3 oz sweet corn, fresh or frozen
2 garlic cloves, minced
1 teaspoon chili powder
1 teaspoon cumin powder
1 cup canned pumpkin puree
1/2 cup wheat germ
1/3 cup breadcrumbs
2 tablespoons all purpose flour
2 tablespoons chopped coriander
Vegan burger buns
Shredded cabbage for serving

Directions:
1. Heat half of the oil in a frying pan or heavy skillet and stir in the onion. Sauté until the onion looks translucent and soft. Mix in the red bell pepper, sweet corn, chili powder, cumin and garlic and cook for 5 minutes, covered with a lid. Transfer into a bowl and let it cool down before proceeding to next step.
2. Stir in the pumpkin puree, breadcrumbs, wheat germ, flour, coriander and a touch of salt and pepper. Mix well to combine. Wet your hands, take spoonfuls of mixture and form small burgers.
3. Heat the remaining oil in a large enough frying pan and cook each burger on both sides for 4-5 minutes until browned and crisp on the surface, but soft and juicy on the inside.
4. Serve the burgers on buns with shredded cabbage as garnish.

Green Lentil and Almond Burgers

Lentils are similar in taste and texture to beans, but much easier to cook. They add lots of flavor to these burgers, together with the delicate aroma of the almonds.

Servings: 6-8 burgers

Ingredients:

1 cup green lentils
5 cups water
3 tablespoons extra virgin olive oil
1 large carrot, peeled and finely chopped
1 shallot, chopped
2 garlic cloves, minced
1 celery stick, finely chopped
1/4 cup sliced almonds
1 tablespoon flax seeds, ground
2 tablespoons water
Salt, pepper

Directions:
1. Pour the water into a large pot and add a pinch of salt. Bring to boiling point then mix in the lentils. Cook for 20 minutes until the lentils absorb most of the liquid and become soft. Set them aside to cool down before proceeding to the next step.
2. Mix the ground flax seeds with the 2 tablespoons of water in a small bowl and set them aside.
3. Heat the 3 tablespoons of oil in a large heavy skillet and stir in the shallot. Cook for 2 minutes to soften it, then add the garlic and sauté 2 more minutes on low heat.
4. Stir in the carrot and celery and cook until they are soft, about 7-8 minutes, stirring frequently.
5. Put half of the lentils in a food processor and pulse until a smooth paste forms. Transfer it into a bowl. Add the remaining lentils, the flax seeds, the shallot and carrot mixture and the sliced almonds. Mix well to combine them all.
6. Wet your hands and form small patties. Put them aside.
7. Heat a small amount of vegetable oil in a frying pan and cook the burgers on each side until they form a golden brown crust on the surface, but remain juicy and soft on the inside. It will take about 4-5 minutes on each side, on low to medium heat.
8. Serve them on vegan burger buns with your favorite toppings

Mediterranean Burgers

Flavorful and packed with lots of nutrients, these burgers are simply delicious as the ingredients they use are high quality and aromatic.

Servings: 8-10 burgers

Ingredients:

1/4 cup sun-dried tomatoes, drained
1 cup water
1/2 cup millet, rinsed
1 1/2 cup vegetable stock
1/4 cup extra virgin olive oil
1 small onion, chopped
2 garlic cloves, minced
4 cups baby spinach leaves
2 tablespoons chopped fresh basil
1/2 cup breadcrumbs
1/2 cup firm tofu, crumbled
Salt, pepper
Vegan burger buns
Arugula and tomato slices to garnish

Directions:
1. Pour the water in a pan and throw in the sun-dried tomatoes. Bring to a boil and set them aside to soak for 1 hour. Drain, then chop them finely.
2. Pour the vegetable stock in another pot and bring to a boil. Stir in the millet and simmer on low heat for 25 minutes until all the liquid has been absorbed. Transfer into a bowl and let it cool before use.
3. Heat 2 tablespoons olive oil in a pan and stir in the onion and garlic. Sauté for 4-5 minutes on low heat until soft and translucent. Stir in the spinach and cook for 1 more minute. Remove from heat and put it in the bowl, with the millet.
4. When the mixture is cold, put it in a food processor or blender and pulse until it's well blended. Transfer back into the bowl and stir in the crumbled tofu, basil, breadcrumbs, tomatoes and a pinch of salt and pepper if needed. Mix to combine well then form small patties. Set them aside until frying.
5. Heat the remaining olive oil in a frying pan and cook the burgers 4-5 minutes on each side until they form a golden brown crust on the outside, but remain soft and juicy on the inside.
6. Serve on vegan burger buns with fresh arugula salad and tomato slices to garnish.

Pecan and Mushroom Burgers

With a strong earthy and nutty flavor, these burgers will surely become a personal favorite. They are nutritious and filling and have that perfect creamy, but chunky at the same time, texture.

Servings: 6-8 burgers

Ingredients:
1 pound cremini mushrooms
2 tablespoons packed parsley leaves
2 tablespoons olive oil
1 onion, chopped
2 garlic cloves, minced
1 cup breadcrumbs
3 oz pecans
2 teaspoons soy sauce
3 tablespoon tahini sauce
1 teaspoon dried oregano
Salt, pepper
Oil for frying

Directions:
1. Put the mushrooms and pecans in a food processor or blender and pulse until well combined and ground. Transfer into a bowl and set aside.
2. Heat the olive oil in a frying pan and sauté the onion until translucent then stir in the garlic and cook until fragrant. Put this mixture in the bowl with the mushrooms and mix in the breadcrumbs, followed by the soy sauce, tahini paste, chopped parsley and dried oregano. Mix to combine well then form little patties. Set them aside.
3. Heat a small quantity of vegetable oil and cook the burgers on each side until they form a golden brown crust. Serve on vegan burger buns with your favorite toppings.

Soybean Burgers

Soy is a great alternative to meat as it has a high content of proteins and fiber. Plus, it tastes great combined with other ingredients, such as vegetables and herbs.

Servings: 8-10 burgers

Ingredients:
3 cups canned soybeans, drained
6 oz firm tofu
1 onion, chopped
1 celery stalk, chopped
1 1/2 cup rolled oats
1/2 teaspoon nutritional yeast
2 tablespoons flax seeds, ground
6 tablespoons water
2 tablespoons wheat gluten
1 teaspoon soy sauce
1 tablespoon olive oil
Salt, pepper

Directions:
1. In a small bowl, whisk together the ground flax seeds with water and set aside.
2. Put the soybeans, tofu, olive oil and yeast in a food processor or blender and pulse a few times until well combined and smooth. Transfer into a bowl. Stir in the celery, onion, flax seeds, rolled oats, yeast, gluten and soy sauce, and mix well. Adjust the taste with a touch of salt and pepper then wet your hands and form small patties. Set them aside.
3. Heat 1/4 cup of vegetable oil in a large frying pan or skillet and cook the burgers on each side for 4-5 minutes or until they form a golden brown crust.
4. Serve them on vegan burger buns with your favorite toppings

Roasted Bell Pepper and Lentil Burgers

Bell peppers are sweet, but flavorful and make a great team with lentils to create a delicious, incredibly tasty vegan burger.

Servings: 8-10 burgers

Ingredients:
4 cups cooked lentils
1 red onion, chopped
2 garlic cloves, minced
2 bell peppers, roasted and peeled
2 tablespoons fresh parsley, chopped
1/2 cup breadcrumbs
1 teaspoon smoked paprika
1 teaspoon cumin
1 teaspoon nutritional yeast
2 tablespoons flax seeds, ground
6 tablespoons water
Salt, pepper
Oil for frying

Directions:
1. Whisk together the flax seeds with water and set aside.
2. Put 2 cups of lentils, roasted bell peppers and spices in a food processor and pulse to combine. Transfer into a bowl and stir in the remaining lentils, flax seeds, nutritional yeast, garlic, onion, parsley and breadcrumbs. Mix well and adjust the taste with salt and pepper. Wet your hands and form small patties. Set them aside.
3. Heat a small quantity of oil in a frying pan or skillet and fry the burgers on each side for 4-5 minutes, on low to medium heat, until golden brown and crusty. Serve on vegan burger buns with your favorite toppings.

Zucchini and Carrot Burgers

Simple, but delicious, these burgers only have a few ingredients but are impressive with their simplicity and incredible taste.

Servings: 4-6 burgers

Ingredients:
1 zucchini, grated
1 carrot, peeled and grated
3 tablespoons flour
Salt, freshly ground pepper

Directions:
1. Put the grated zucchini and carrot in a bowl and stir in the flour. Add a pinch of salt and freshly ground pepper and mix to combine well.
2. Heat a small quantity of vegetable oil in a pan and drop spoonfuls of batter into the hot oil. Cook on each side for 3-4 minutes then remove onto paper towels.
3. Serve simply, on vegan burger buns or with some tomato slices

Sweet Potato and Basil Burgers

The best combinations come from those that seem unusual. This recipe combines the sweetness of the sweet potatoes with the aromatic basil to create a delicious, creamy burger for your everyday meals.

Servings: 2-4 burgers

Ingredients:
2 sweet potatoes, washed
4 tablespoons fresh chopped basil
2 tablespoons rolled oats
2 tablespoons whole wheat flour
1 green onion, chopped
Salt, pepper

Directions:
1. Wrap the 2 potatoes in foil and cook them in the oven at medium heat for 30-40 minutes or until tender. Scoop out the flesh into a bowl and mash it with a fork. Stir in the basil, green onion, oats and flour, and mix well to combine.
2. Add a small amount of oil in a pan and heat it up. Drop spoonfuls of burger batter in the hot oil and cook, flipping once, for 5-6 minutes or until slightly golden brown.
3. Serve on vegan burger buns with your favorite toppings

Sun-dried Tomatoes and Black Bean Burgers

Packing summer flavors, these burgers are creamy, flavorful and a bit spicy, just enough to awaken your senses.

Servings: 8-10 burgers

Ingredients:
4 oz sun-dried tomatoes
2 cups warm water
3 cups canned black beans, drained
1 teaspoon cumin
1/2 teaspoon dried oregano
2 tablespoons fresh chopped basil
1 cup rolled oats
1 cup cooked brown rice
Salt, pepper

Directions:
1. In a bowl, mix the sun-dried tomatoes with the warm water and let them soak for 30 minutes then chop them finely.
2. Put the beans in a food processor and pulse until smooth. Transfer into a bowl and stir in the chopped tomatoes, cumin, oregano, basil, as well as oats and brown rice. Adjust the taste with salt and pepper and form small patties. Set them aside while you heat your grill or grill pan.
3. Cook each burger on both sides for 5-6 minutes or more, until crusty and slightly browned.
4. Serve on vegan burger buns, simply or with your favorite toppings.

Spicy Spinach and Tofu Burgers

Moist and delicious, these burgers are a great way to cook spinach or tofu when you seem bored of the classic soups or stews.

Servings: 4-6 burgers

Ingredients:
3 cups frozen spinach, thawed and drained
2 tablespoons flax seeds, ground
4 tablespoons water
1 onion, finely chopped
4 oz tofu, crumbled
1/2 cup breadcrumbs
2 garlic cloves, minced
1/4 teaspoon cayenne pepper
Salt

Directions:
1. In a small bowl, mix the ground flax seeds with water.
2. Squeeze the spinach with your hands to remove any water. Put into a bowl and stir in the onion, crumbled tofu, breadcrumbs, garlic, pepper and flax seeds. Adjust the taste with salt and pepper. Wet or grease your hands and form small burgers.
3. Cook them in a hot pan with a small amount of vegetable oil. They should be crusty and slightly golden brown, but moist on the inside.

Chapter 3: Baked Burgers

Baked burgers have the huge advantage of being healthier as they do not require any oil to be cooked, but they do take more time to make and the cooking process can be more complex sometimes. However, the recipes included in this chapter try to be as straight forward as possible without sacrificing any taste. You will find a bunch of good recipes to try, healthy and delicious, using only flavorful ingredients, specially chosen to fit your vegan lifestyle.

Sweet Potato and Parsley Burgers

Creamy and delicious, these burgers are also very fragrant because of adding parsley, but also easy to make and filling. These burgers are perfect for either lunch or dinner or, why not, a snack between meals.

Servings: 4-6 burgers

Ingredients:
2 sweet potatoes, peeled and cubed
1 cup rolled oats
3 green onions, finely chopped
1/2 cup chopped parsley
Salt, pepper

Directions:
1. Put the potato cubes in a steamer and cook them until tender. Transfer them into a bowl and mash them with a fork. Stir in the rest of ingredients then form small patties with your wet hands as the mixture tends to be sticky.
2. Arrange the burgers in a pan lined with parchment paper then bake them in the preheated oven at 400° F until golden brown and crusty.
3. Serve them on Vegan burger buns with tomato slices or vegan yogurt and garlic sauce.

Basil and Quinoa Burgers

Basil is an aromatic plant mostly used in Italian cuisine, but nowadays it is known worldwide because of its unique aroma and the capability to change a common dish into a stunning one. This burger may be simple, but the basil makes it worth the time spent in making it because the end result is simply delicious.

Servings: 6-8 burgers

Ingredients:
2 teaspoons flax seeds, ground
4 tablespoons water
1 1/2 cup canned white beans, drained
1 1/2 cups cooked quinoa
2 red potatoes, cubed, boiled, and mashed
1 teaspoon nutritional yeast
1 small red onion, finely chopped
2 tablespoons all purpose flour
2 garlic cloves
1/2 cup packed fresh basil, chopped
Salt, pepper

Directions:
1. Mix the ground flax seeds with water and set them aside. Flax seeds are a vegan alternative to eggs and grinding them then mixing them with water makes sure we get a similar texture to egg as they transform into a gel.
2. Put the beans in a food processor and pulse to purée them. Transfer them into a large bowl then stir in the soaked flax seeds, quinoa, mashed potatoes, basil, nutritional yeast, flour and chopped onion plus minced garlic. Mix well then adjust the taste with a touch of pepper and salt.
3. Wet or grease your hands, take spoonfuls of mixture and form the burgers. Set them aside while you heat your oven to 375º F. Arrange all the burgers in a pan lined with parchment paper and bake them in the oven for 40 minutes until golden brown.

Stuffed Portobello Burgers with Onion Marmalade

Portobello mushrooms are perfect for grilling, not only because of their size but also because of their earthy flavor and texture. Try stuffing them with other vegetables and serve them with a delicious onion jam on a burger bun. It is simply delicious.

Servings: 4 burgers

Ingredients:
4 Portobello mushrooms
1 small zucchini, diced
1 onion, finely chopped
1 tomato, peeled, deseeded, and diced
2 tablespoons packed basil leaves, chopped
Salt, pepper
For the onion marmalade:
3 red onions, sliced
1 cup sugar
1/2 cup vinegar
1 cinnamon stick
Vegan burger buns

Directions:
1. In a bowl, mix the diced zucchini, onion, tomato and basil. Arrange the mushrooms in a baking pan and spoon the filling into each of them. Cook in the oven for 25 minutes, at 375º F
2. In the meantime, make the marmalade. Put the onion, sugar, vinegar and cinnamon stick in a saucepan over a medium flame. Bring to a boil then lower the heat and simmer until almost all the liquid has evaporated and the marmalade looks thick and fragrant.
3. When the stuffed Portobello are ready, serve them on vegan burger buns with a dollop of onion marmalade.

Bulgur and Parsley Baked Burgers

Bulgur is a very healthy grain so, as a vegan, you might want to include it in your diet because of its high fiber and protein content, not to mention how delicious it is.

Serving: 6-8 burgers

Ingredients:
4 cups water
1 1/4 cup uncooked bulgur
2 cups chopped parsley leaves
1 cucumber, diced
1 tomato, peeled, deseeded, and diced
2 tablespoons chopped mint leaves
4 tablespoons olive oil
3 garlic cloves, minced
Juice from 1/2 lemon
2 tablespoons cornstarch
1 cup whole wheat flour
Whole wheat Vegan burger buns
Tzatziki sauce for serving

Directions:
1. Pour the water into a large pot and add a pinch of salt. Bring to a boil then stir in the bulgur. Simmer on low heat for 15 minutes or until all the liquid has been absorbed. Set aside to cool before proceeding to next step.
2. Take a large bowl and add the parsley, mint, cucumber, tomato, garlic, lemon juice, olive oil and salt and pepper to taste. Mix well then stir in the flour and cornstarch. Wet your hands and form small burgers. Arrange all of them on a baking tray lined with parchment paper.
3. Bake them in the preheated oven at 375º F for 40 minutes or until crusty and golden brown.
4. Serve on vegan burger buns with tzatziki sauce as garnish.

Spinach Tofu Burgers

Homemade burgers will always be better than store bought ones mainly because, at home, you have full control over which vegetables you use and what condiments you add. This particular recipe combines spinach and tofu with walnuts and brown rice. It is healthy and fairly easy to make.

Servings: 6-8 burgers

Ingredients:
10 oz fresh spinach, chopped
2 tablespoons olive oil
1 leek, finely chopped
1 carrot, peeled and grated
2 garlic cloves, minced
1 teaspoon dried oregano
1/4 cup walnuts
1/4 cup cooked brown rice
1 package firm tofu, crumbled
2 tablespoons fresh chopped dill
Salt, pepper to taste

Directions:
1. Heat the olive oil in a pan and stir in the leeks, carrot, garlic and dried oregano. Sauté 3-4 minutes then add the spinach and cook 1 more minute until it's softened. Remove from heat and set aside.
2. Put the tofu and walnuts in a food processor and pulse until well combined. Add half of the spinach and pulse a few more times to combine. Put the mixture into a bowl and stir in the remaining spinach.
3. Mix in the brown rice, chopped dill and salt and pepper to taste. Mix well then form burgers. Arrange them on a baking tray lined with parchment paper and bake in the preheated oven at 350º F until it forms a golden crust, about 40 minutes.
4. Serve on vegan burger buns with your favorite toppings.

Baked Sweet Corn Tofu Burgers

Sweet corn is very often used to make patties, not just burgers because it has an interesting texture. Combined with tofu, they yield a delicious, flavorful burger you will love.

Servings: 8-10 burgers

Ingredients:
1 cup frozen sweet corn
1/2 cup walnuts
1 package firm tofu, crumbled
2 garlic cloves
1 carrot, peeled and grated
1/2 cup cornmeal
1/2 cup flour
1 tablespoon tahini paste
2 tablespoons chopped coriander
1 teaspoon cumin powder
salt, pepper

Directions:
1. Put the walnuts and half of the sweet corn in a food processor, along with the coriander. Pulse a few times until well blended.
2. Transfer into a bowl and stir in the remaining corn, garlic, crumbled tofu, carrot, cornmeal and flour. Add the tahini paste and cumin powder and adjust the taste with salt and pepper.
3. Mix well then form small burgers with your wet hands. Arrange all of them on a baking tray lined with parchment paper and bake in the preheated oven at 350° F for 40 minutes.
4. Serve on vegan burger buns with your favorite toppings.

Herbed Tofu Burger

Spicy and aromatic, this burger will impress you with its earthy flavors, being a very healthy option for any meal of the day because of the high content of fiber and nutrients.

Servings: 8-10 burgers

Ingredients:
15 oz firm tofu, drained well
1 tablespoon dried parsley
2 tablespoons dried basil
1 tablespoons fresh chopped thyme
1 teaspoon dried rosemary
1 cup cooked brown rice
2 garlic cloves, minced
2 tablespoons flax seeds, ground
4 tablespoons water
1/2 cup seeds mix (sunflower, pumpkin)
Salt, pepper

Directions:
1. Mix the flax seeds with water in a small bowl.
2. Crumble the tofu in a large bowl. Stir in the herbs, both fresh and dried ones, and mix well. Add the cooked rice then the minced garlic and flax seeds. Mix in the seeds and combine well. Adjust the taste with salt and pepper and form small patties. Arrange them on a baking tray lined with parchment paper and drizzle olive oil on top.
3. Cook in the preheated oven at 350º F for 20-30 minutes until slightly golden brown and fragrant.
4. Serve on vegan burger buns with your favorite toppings or wrap in foil and freeze for later serving.

Spicy Mushroom and Black-eyed Pea Burgers

Mushrooms and black-eyed peas give these burgers the right texture and consistency as well as moisture, making them incredibly tasty.

Servings: 6-8 burgers

Ingredients:
5 oz cremini mushrooms, thinly sliced
1 red onion, chopped
2 garlic cloves, minced
2 tablespoons olive oil
2 cups canned black-eyed peas
2 tablespoons chopped parsley
1 teaspoon soy sauce
1/2 teaspoon chili flakes
Salt, pepper

Directions:
1. Heat the olive oil in a large pan and stir in the onion. Cook until translucent then add the mushrooms and keep cooking 10 more minutes. Add the garlic then remove from heat into a bowl.
2. Put the peas into a blender and pulse a few times, just to mash them a bit. Put them in the bowl with the mushrooms. Add the soy sauce and chili flakes and mix to combine well. Wet your hands and form small patties.
3. Arrange all of them on a baking tray and cook in the preheated oven at 400º F about 20-30 minutes, just until they start to look golden brown on the surface.
4. Serve on vegan burger buns with your favorite toppings.

Vegetable Flax Seed Burgers

Flax seeds are high in fiber and nutrients; therefore adding them into your diet is a must. The best thing about them is, if ground, they can replace eggs and make any dough come together easier.

Servings: 6-8 burgers

Ingredients:
7 oz artichoke hearts, drained and chopped
2 garlic cloves, minced
2 tablespoons fresh chopped parsley
1 cup canned chickpeas, drained
1 cup canned kidney beans, drained
2 tablespoons tahini paste
1 carrot, peeled and grated
3 tablespoons flax seeds
1/2 cup rolled oats
Salt, pepper

Directions:
1. Simply put all the ingredients into a food processor and pulse a few times until well blended, but not yet transformed into a paste. You want a chunkier texture.
2. Wet your hands and form small patties. Arrange them all on a baking tray lined with parchment paper and cook in the preheated oven at 400° F for 20-30 minutes until slightly golden brown on the surface.
3. Serve on vegan burger buns with tomato slices, lettuce leaves, shredded cabbage, or any other toppings you like.

Carrot and Walnut Burgers

Although carrots may be a bit sweet, combined with the earthy flavor of the walnuts, they yield a delicious, juicy burger you will love.

Servings: 4-6 burgers

Ingredients:
4 carrot, peeled and grated
1 small onion, finely chopped
2 garlic cloves, minced
1 tablespoon olive oil
1 teaspoon cumin
1/2 cup walnuts, chopped
2 tablespoons sunflower seeds
1 cup canned chickpeas
1 cup cooked quinoa
2 tablespoons chopped parsley
Salt, pepper
1/4 cup whole wheat flour

Directions:
1. Heat the olive oil in a small pan and sauté the onion and garlic for 2-3 minutes. Add the cumin and sauté 1 more minute until fragrant.
2. Put the chickpeas in a food processor and pulse until a smooth paste forms. Transfer into a large bowl and stir in the onion mixture, chopped walnuts, sunflower seeds, quinoa, chopped parsley and a pinch of salt and pepper.
3. Wet your hands and form small patties. Coat each burger in whole wheat flour and arrange them on a baking pan lined with parchment paper. Refrigerate for 30 minutes then cook in the preheated oven at 400º F for 30-40 minutes until browned and crusty on the surface.
4. Serve in vegan burger buns with your favorite toppings.

Sesame Seeds and Millet Burgers

Roasted sesame seeds have a strong, earthy flavor but also have a high content of good fats and fibers. Combining them with millet in these burgers can only mean they are delicious and healthier than you may think.

Servings: 6-8 burgers

Ingredients:
1 1/4 cup millet
3 1/2 cups water or vegetable broth
1 carrot, peeled and grated
1 small onion, chopped
2 garlic cloves, minced
2 tablespoons olive oil
1/4 cup breadcrumbs
1 teaspoon Italian seasoning
1/4 cup sesame seeds
Salt, pepper

Directions:
1. Put the millet in a pan and roast it for 3-4 minutes, just to enhance its flavor. Pour the water or broth into a pot and bring to a boil. Stir in the roasted millet and simmer on low heat until all the liquid has been absorbed. Transfer into a bowl and set aside.
2. Heat the oil in a skillet and sauté the onion and garlic for 2 minutes then add it to the bowl. Mix well then stir in the Italian seasoning, breadcrumbs and carrot. Mix to combine well and form small patties. Coat each burger in sesame seeds and arrange all of them on a baking tray lined with parchment paper.
3. Cook in a preheated oven at high heat until golden brown on the surface, about 40 minutes.
4. Serve on vegan burger buns with arugula and tomato slices.

Brown Lentil and Nut Burgers

Rich and moist, these burgers are a delight with their nutty, earthy flavor and fine consistency. They are filling enough to represent a meal on their own, but also very healthy and much more beneficial than regular burgers.

Servings: 8-10 burgers

Ingredients:
1 1/2 cup cooked brown rice
1 1/2 cup canned brown lentils
1 carrot, peeled and grated
1 cup whole wheat breadcrumbs
1/2 cup peanut butter
1/4 cup chopped walnuts
1 teaspoon soy sauce
1 teaspoon dried oregano
2 tablespoons chopped parsley
1 teaspoon smoked paprika
Salt, pepper

Directions:
1. Combine the lentils and cooked rice in a bowl then stir in the carrot, breadcrumbs, peanut butter, walnuts, parsley and the spices.
2. Mix well to combine then adjust the taste with salt and pepper. Wet your hands and form small burgers. Arrange them on a baking tray lined with parchment paper and cook in a preheated oven at 400º F for 30 minutes.
3. Serve on vegan burger buns with your favorite toppings.

Baked Falafel Burgers

Falafel is, in fact, a vegan burger, but cooked in the form of small patties. It is usually fried, but baking it is much healthier as it uses far less oil, but the flavors are the same.

Servings: 6-8 burgers

Ingredients:
2 cups canned chickpeas, drained
1 small onion, chopped
1/3 cup chopped coriander
1 teaspoon cumin
1 teaspoon lemon juice
2 tablespoons flour
2 tablespoons olive oil
Salt, pepper

Directions:
1. Put all the ingredients in a food processor and pulse a few times until it comes together but it's not a paste. The texture has to be slightly chunkier.
2. Wet your hands and form small burgers. Arrange them all on a baking tray lined with parchment paper and cook them in the preheated oven at 400º F until golden brown on the surface and cooked through, about 30-40 minutes.
3. Serve on vegan burger buns with your favorite toppings.

Lentil and Pesto Burgers

Pesto is an Italian aromatic sauce made mainly with basil. It has a strong flavor, therefore it works great with milder aromas at its side, such as these simple lentil burgers.

Servings: 8-10 burgers

Ingredients:
2 cups canned lentils, drained
1 green onion, chopped
1 garlic clove, minced
1/2 cup rolled oats
1 tablespoon flour
1/8 teaspoon cayenne pepper
1 cup packed basil leaves
1/2 cup pine nuts
4 tablespoons olive oil
1 teaspoon lemon juice
Salt, pepper

Directions:
1. Put the half of the lentils, the onion and garlic in a food processor. Pulse a few times until a smooth paste forms then transfer into a bowl.
2. Stir in the remaining lentils, rolled oats and flour and adjust the taste with salt and pepper. Wet your hands and form small burgers. Arrange all of them on a baking tray lined with parchment paper and bake in the preheated oven at 400º F until golden brown and crusty.
3. In the meantime, make the pesto: Put the basil leaves, pine nuts and lemon juice in a small blender or food processor and pulse, adding the olive oil gradually. Blend until smooth.
4. Serve the burgers on buns with a dollop of pesto.

Smoky Beetroot Burgers

Delicate and flavorful, these burgers are also very colorful and preserve a mild smoky flavor from the smoked paprika used to make them.

Servings: 4-6 burgers

Ingredients:
1 small onion, chopped
2 tablespoons olive oil
2/3 cup walnuts
1/2 cup raisins
1 beetroot, peeled and grated
1 teaspoon smoked paprika
1/2 cup canned lentils, drained
1 tablespoon flax seeds, ground
3 tablespoons water
1 2/3 cups cooked brown rice
Salt, pepper

Directions:
1. Whisk the ground flax seeds with water and set aside. Heat the olive oil in a heavy skillet and sauté the onion for 5 minutes until translucent. Add the garlic, walnuts, raisins, beetroots and paprika, and keep cooking 10 more minutes. Transfer into a food processor and pulse a few times until well blended, but still slightly chunky.
2. Transfer into a bowl and stir in the flax seeds, cooked brown rice and a pinch of salt and pepper. Wet your hands and form small patties. Arrange them on a baking tray lined with parchment paper and cook in the preheated oven at 400° F until crusty and slightly browned on the surface. It will take about 30-40 minutes.
3. Serve on vegan burger buns with tomato slices, arugula or lettuce and cucumber slices.

Pumpkin Black Beans Burgers

Rich and filling, these burgers pack some lovely autumn flavors and create a delicious burger to enjoy at every time of the day.

Servings: 6-8 burgers

Ingredients:
2/3 cup pumpkin puree, canned
2 garlic cloves
1 cup cooked brown rice
2 cups black beans
1 teaspoon cumin
1/2 teaspoon chili powder
2 tablespoons flax seeds, ground
1/2 cup rolled oats
1/4 cup breadcrumbs
2 tablespoons pumpkin seeds
Salt, pepper

Directions:
1. Put the black beans in a food processor and pulse a few times until smooth. Transfer into a bowl and stir in the pumpkin purée , garlic, brown rice, cumin, chili and flax seeds, followed by the rolled oats, breadcrumbs and pumpkin seeds.
2. Adjust the taste with salt and pepper and form small burgers. Arrange them all on a baking tray and cook in the preheated oven for 30-40 minutes or until browned and crisp on the surface.
3. Serve on vegan burger buns with your favorite toppings.

Kale and Oatmeal Burgers

Kale is very similar to spinach, but it has a milder flavor. Therefore, it can be consumed even by those who don't usually tolerate spinach.

Servings: 4-6 burgers

Ingredients:
2 cups canned white beans, drained
2 garlic cloves
1 onion, finely chopped
2 tablespoons olive oil
2 cups chopped kale
1 teaspoon lemon juice
1 cup rolled oats
Salt, pepper

Directions:
1. Heat the olive oil in a large pan and stir in the onion. Cook for 5-7 minutes until slightly browned then stir in the garlic and kale. Cook 1-2 minutes until they start to soften then set aside.
2. Put the white beans in a food processor and pulse a few times until smooth. Transfer into a bowl and stir in the kale mixture, as well as the rolled oats and lemon juice. Mix well then wet your hands and form small patties. Arrange them all on a baking tray and cook in the preheated oven at 400º F for 20-30 minutes.
3. Serve on vegan burger buns with tomato slices and a sprinkle of smoked paprika.

Green Lentils and Sunflower Seed Burgers with Garlic Sauce

Easy to make, these burgers are great served with a garlic sauce, on fresh vegan burger buns.

Servings: 4-6 burgers

Ingredients:
2 cups canned green lentils, drained and rinsed
2 tablespoons olive oil
1 green onion, chopped
1 garlic clove, chopped
1 carrot, peeled and grated
1/2 cup sunflower seeds
1/2 cup breadcrumbs
2 tablespoons rolled oats
Salt, pepper
For the sauce:
1/2 cup vegan yogurt
1/2 teaspoon ginger
2 garlic cloves

Directions:
1. Put the lentils in a food processor and pulse until well blended. Transfer into a bowl and stir in the onion, garlic, carrot, seeds, breadcrumbs and rolled oats. Adjust the taste with salt and pepper and form small patties with your wet or greased hands. Place the burgers on a baking tray lined with parchment paper and refrigerate 30 minutes.
2. In the meantime, preheat your oven at 400º F. Bake the burgers for 30-40 minutes or until crisp and golden brown on the outside.
3. To make the sauce, mix the 3 ingredients in a small bowl.

Baked Sesame Tofu Burgers

Using black sesame seeds and herbed tofu, these burgers are delicious and moist with a strong earthy flavor and a chunky, but silky texture.

Servings: 4-6 burgers

Ingredients:
1/2 cup chopped green onions
1 pound herbed firm tofu
1/2 cup breadcrumbs
1/2 cup black sesame seeds
1 teaspoon soy sauce
1 teaspoon fresh grated ginger
3 oz sushi wrapping
Salt, pepper

Directions:
1. Pour 2 cups of water into a pot and bring to a boil. Remove from heat and stir in the sushi wrap. Set aside to soak then drain well.
2. Put half of the tofu in a food processor. Add green onion and sushi wrap and pulse a few times until well blended. Transfer into a bowl and stir in the breadcrumbs, soy sauce and fresh ginger, as well as a pinch of salt and freshly ground pepper. Wet or grease your hands and form small burgers. Coat each burger in black sesame seeds and arrange them all on a baking tray lined with parchment paper.
3. Preheat your oven to 375° F and cook the burgers for 20-40 minutes, until slightly golden brown and fragrant.
4. Serve on vegan burger buns with any topping you like, from arugula and tomato slices to shredded cabbage or cucumbers.

Roasted Red Pepper and Eggplant Burgers

Roasting the pepper only enhances their taste and adds a smoky touch that works great with the eggplant. The end result is a creamy, fragrant burger that is perfect served with tomato slices.

Servings: 4-6 burgers

Ingredients:
2 red bell peppers, roasted and peeled
1 eggplant
1 teaspoon cumin
1 tablespoon olive oil
1/2 cup rolled oats
2/3 cup whole wheat breadcrumbs
2 tablespoons chopped parsley
2 tablespoons chopped coriander
Salt, pepper
Vegan burger buns
Tomato slices

Directions:
1. Cut the eggplant in half, put it in a baking pan, drizzle with olive oil and sprinkle with cumin. Bake in the preheated oven at 350° F for 30 minutes, until soft. Scoop the flesh out into a bowl.
2. Finely chop the bell peppers and mix them into the bowl. Add the oats, breadcrumbs, parsley and coriander. Adjust the taste with salt and pepper and set aside 30 minutes.
3. Wet your hands and form small burgers. Arrange them on a baking tray lined with parchment paper and cook in the oven at 350° F until golden brown.
4. Serve on vegan burger buns with tomato slices.

Oatmeal and Beetroot Burgers with Barley Salad

Colorful and as healthy as possible, these burgers are also easy to make and have a unique earthy flavor from the beetroot. They are moist and juicy, great for any meal of the day.

Servings: 6-8 burgers

Ingredients:

For burgers:
2 beetroots, peeled and grated
1 cup rolled oats
1 cup canned chickpeas, drained
1 tablespoon fresh chopped dill
1 tablespoon fresh chopped parsley
1 teaspoon fresh chopped thyme
2 green onions, finely chopped
Salt, pepper

For salad:
1 cup barley
1 celery stalk, sliced
1 cup chopped parsley
2 teaspoons balsamic vinegar
1 tablespoon olive oil

Directions:

To make the burgers:

1. Put the chickpeas in a food processor or blender and pulse until a smooth paste forms. Transfer into a bowl and stir in the rolled oats, grated beets, dill, parsley, thyme and green onions.
2. Adjust the taste with salt and pepper and form small patties. Place the burgers on a baking tray lined with parchment paper and cook in the preheated oven at 375° F for 30-40 minutes until cooked through.

To make the salad:
1. Put the barley in a bowl together with the celery and parsley. Mix the vinegar with olive oil and stir it in, tossing well to evenly coat.
2. Serve the burgers on buns, topped with barley salad.

Potato and Bean Burgers with Garlic Aioli

Potato and beans must be some of the most common ingredients found in everyone's pantry and if you didn't think on combining them so far, think again.

Servings: 6-8 burgers

Ingredients:
1 pound potatoes, washed
1 cup canned white beans
2 tablespoons fresh chopped dill
1/2 teaspoon fresh chopped thyme
1/2 cup rolled oats
1 carrot, peeled and grated
Salt, pepper

Directions:
1. Wrap the potatoes in foil and cook them in the oven until tender. When done, scoop out the flesh into a bowl and stir in the dill, thyme, rolled oats and carrot. Season with salt and pepper.
2. Put the white beans in a bowl and mash them with a potato masher then add them to the bowl as well.
3. Mix well to combine then form small burgers. Arrange them all on a baking tray lined with parchment paper and cook in the preheated oven at 375º F until slightly golden, about 20-30 minutes.
4. To make the garlic aioli, simply mix 1/2 cup vegan yogurt with 3 minced garlic cloves and a pinch of salt and freshly ground pepper.
5. Serve the burgers on buns with a spoonful of aioli.

Courgette Burgers

Courgettes have a taste similar to zucchini, but they are juicy and silky and simply delicious in these burgers.

Servings: 6-8 burgers

Ingredients:
2 courgettes, grated
2 garlic cloves, minced
1 tablespoon flax seeds, ground
2/3 cup breadcrumbs
1 teaspoon Italian seasoning
3 tablespoons all purpose flour
Salt, pepper
2 tablespoons olive oil

Directions:
1. Mix the flax seeds with 2 tablespoons of water and set aside to soak.
2. Combine the grated courgettes with breadcrumbs, Italian seasoning, flour and garlic, then stir in the flax seeds. Mix well then form small patties.
3. Arrange them all on a baking tray and drizzle them with a bit of olive oil. Cook in a preheated oven at 375° F for 20-30 minutes or until slightly golden brown.
4. Serve on vegan burger buns with your favorite toppings

Crispy Chickpea Burgers

Crisp on the outside but moist and juicy on the inside, these burgers can be the star of any meal. They are healthy and highly nutritious, but easy to make at the same time.

Servings: 6-8 burgers

Ingredients:
1 onion, chopped
1 celery stalk, chopped
2 tablespoons olive oil
3 cups canned chickpeas, drained and rinsed
1 teaspoon fresh chopped thyme
1 teaspoon cayenne pepper
3 tablespoons chopped parsley
2 tablespoons flour
Salt, pepper

Directions:
1. Heat the oil in a heavy skillet. Stir in the onion and celery and sauté for 5 minutes. Transfer into a blender and add the chickpeas. Pulse until well blended, but still a bit chunky. Put this mixture into a bowl and stir in the thyme, pepper, parsley and flour.
2. Adjust the taste with salt and pepper then wet or grease your hands and form small patties. Arrange them all on a baking tray and cook in a preheated oven at 350º F for 30-40 minutes until crisp on the outside.
3. Serve on vegan burger buns with your favorite toppings.

Broccoli and Lentil Baked Burgers

Probably one of the easiest vegan burgers out there, this recipe also yields some delicious, moist patties that will impress even the pickiest eaters.

Servings: 6-8 burgers

Ingredients:
1 cup canned beans, drained
1/2 cup cooked peas
1 tomato, peeled, deseeded, and finely diced
1 head broccoli, shredded
1/2 cup pumpkin puree
1 tablespoon flour
Salt, pepper

Directions:
1. Put the beans and peas in a bowl and purée them with a potato masher. Stir in the tomato, shredded broccoli, pumpkin purée and flour.
2. Adjust the taste with salt and freshly ground pepper then form small patties. Arrange all of them on a baking tray lined with parchment paper and cook in a preheated oven at 350º F for 30-40 minutes until slightly golden brown.
3. Serve on vegan burger buns with a lettuce leaf and a simple garlic sauce made with a little vegan yogurt and a touch of minced garlic.

Tofu Tempeh Burger

Like tofu, tempeh is made from soy beans. It is nutritious and healthy and adding it into your vegan diet is a great idea.

Servings: 6-8 burgers

Ingredients:
10 oz plain tempeh
1 cup flour
3 tablespoons almond butter
1 tablespoon maple syrup
3 tablespoons peanut butter
1/2 teaspoon smoked paprika
Salt, pepper

Directions:
1. Put the tempeh in a bowl and crumble it into small bits. Stir in the flour, butter, maple syrup, peanut butter and paprika. Adjust the taste with salt and pepper and mix well until it comes together. Wet your hands and form small patties.
2. Arrange them on a baking tray and cook them in the oven at 375° F for 20-30 minutes or until slightly golden brown.
3. Serve on vegan burger buns with ketchup or your favorite toppings.

Tabbouleh Burgers

Tabbouleh is a Lebanese salad consisting of lots of fresh herbs, bulgur, tomatoes, and cucumber. This recipe uses all those lovely ingredients to create a delicious burger you will surely love.

Servings: 8-10 burgers

Ingredients:
1 cup uncooked bulgur
3 cups water or vegetable broth
3 cups fresh chopped parsley
1 cup fresh chopped coriander
1/4 cup fresh chopped mint
3 tomatoes, peeled, deseeded, and diced
4 garlic cloves, minced
1 cucumber, diced
juice from 1/2 lemon
1 cup whole wheat flour
1/4 cup cornstarch
2 tablespoons olive oil.
Salt, pepper

Directions:
1. Pour the water into a pot and bring to a boil. Stir in the bulgur and cook on a low heat until all the liquid has been absorbed. Transfer into a bowl and stir in the herbs, tomatoes, cucumber, garlic and lemon juice, followed by the whole wheat flour, cornstarch and olive oil, as well as a pinch of salt and pepper. Mix well until a batter comes together.
2. Wet your hands and form small burgers. Arrange all of them on a baking tray lined with parchment paper and cook them in the preheated oven at 375º F for 40-50 minutes until slightly browned and fragrant. Serve them on vegan burger buns with a few tomato slices and lettuce leaves.

Cauliflower and Broccoli Burgers

Similar in taste and texture, broccoli and cauliflower taste great together especially in this rich, filling burger.

Servings: 8-10 burgers

Ingredients:
1/2 head cauliflower, cut into florets
1/2 head broccoli, cut into florets
1 carrot, peeled and grated
1/2 teaspoon dried oregano
1 teaspoon dried basil
1/2 cup rolled oats
1/2 cup all purpose flour
2 tablespoons olive oil
1/2 teaspoon hot sauce
Salt, pepper
2 tablespoons flax seeds
4 tablespoons water
Shredded cabbage
Vegan burger buns

Directions:
1. Mix the flax seeds and water in a small bowl. Set aside to soak.
2. Put the broccoli and cauliflower in a steamer and cook 15-20 minutes or until tender. Transfer into a bowl and mash them with a potato masher. Stir in the grated carrot, dried herbs, rolled oats, flour, oil, hot sauce and flax seeds.
3. Mix well then adjust the taste with a pinch of salt and freshly ground pepper. Take spoonfuls of the mixture and form burgers. Arrange them all on a baking tray and cook them in a preheated oven at 375º F for 30-40 minutes.
4. Serve them on vegan burger buns with some shredded cabbage.

Fava Bean Burgers

Similar in texture to soybeans, fava beans are a great choice for any meal for vegans. They are very versatile and can make a great soup, as well as stew and burgers.

Servings: 6-8 burgers

Ingredients:
8 oz fava beans, frozen
1 cup cooked quinoa
1 carrot, grated
1/2 cup rolled oats
2 green onions, finely chopped
1 garlic clove, minced
2 tablespoons flour
Salt, pepper

Directions:
1. Pour a few cups of water in a large pot and bring to a boil. Stir in the fava beans and cook them for 15-20 minutes. Drain them and put them in a blender or food processor. Pulse them until smooth.
2. Transfer into a bowl and stir in the cooked quinoa, flour, onions, garlic and rolled oats. Taste and add salt and pepper if needed. Wet your hands and form small patties. Arrange them all on a baking tray lined with parchment paper.
3. Heat your oven to 375° F and cook the burgers for 30-40 minutes. They should be slightly golden brown and crisp on the surface.
4. Serve them on vegan burger buns, topped with tomato slices and arugula or baby spinach leaves.

Leek and Cauliflower Burgers

Moist and flavorful, these burgers pack the sweet taste of the cauliflower with the unique aroma of the leeks to create an incredibly delicious burger, creamy and filling.

Servings: 4-6 burgers

Ingredients:

1 cauliflower head, trimmed and cut into florets
2 leeks, finely sliced
1 carrot, peeled and grated
2 tablespoons olive oil
1/2 teaspoon dried thyme
1/2 teaspoon dried oregano
1/2 cup rolled oats
1/2 cup all purpose flour
Salt, pepper

Directions:

1. Heat the oil in a heavy skillet and sauté the leeks for 5-8 minutes or until soft. Set aside.
2. Put the cauliflower florets in a steamer and cook for 10-15 minutes until tender. Transfer into a bowl and mash them with a potato masher. Stir in the cooked leeks, thyme, oregano, rolled oats and flour, as well as a pinch of salt and freshly ground pepper to taste.
3. Mix well until it comes together then form patties. Arrange all of them on baking trays lined with parchment paper.
4. Preheat your oven to 375º F and cook the burgers for 30-40 minutes or until crusty and browned, but still juicy and moist on the inside.
5. Serve on vegan burger buns with your favorite toppings

Baked Garlic and Bean Burgers

By baking the garlic first, we enhance its natural sweetness and flavors. It is then mixed with mashed beans to create a delicious burger that can be served with any toppings you like.

Servings: 6-8 burgers

Ingredients:
2 garlic heads
2 onions, chopped
3 cups canned white beans, drained and rinsed
3 tablespoons olive oil
1 teaspoon dried thyme
1 teaspoon smoked paprika
1 cup cooked quinoa
2 tablespoons all purpose flour
Salt, pepper

Directions:
1. Heat the oil in a heavy skillet and sauté the onions for 8-10 minutes or until it starts to look browned. Set aside.
2. Cut the garlic heads in half lengthwise and wrap them in foil. Cook them in the oven at 350F until soft. Remove from oven and scoop the flesh out into a bowl.
3. Put the beans and garlic in a food processor and pulse a few times until smooth. Transfer into a bowl and stir in the cooked onions, thyme, paprika, quinoa and flour. Adjust the taste with salt and freshly ground pepper to taste and mix well.
4. Wet your hands and form burgers. Arrange all of them on baking trays lined with parchment paper and cook in the oven at 350° F for 30-40 minutes.
5. Serve on vegan burger buns with your favorite toppings.

Chickpea and Tempeh Burgers

Made of soy beans, tempeh is pretty dry so it works well with ingredients that keep the moisture in the burgers, like chickpeas and beans.

Servings: 8-10 burgers

Ingredients:
1 cup canned chickpeas, drained
2 cups canned white beans, drained
1 cup tempeh, crumbled
1 teaspoon cumin
1 tablespoon soy sauce
2 tablespoons tahini paste
2 green onions, chopped
3/4 cup rolled oats
Salt, pepper

Directions:
1. Put the chickpeas and white beans in a food processor and pulse a few times until well blended but not yet a paste. Transfer into a bowl and stir in the crumbled tempeh, cumin, soy sauce, tahini paste, green onions and rolled oats, as well as salt and freshly ground pepper to taste.
2. Wet or grease your hands and form small patties. Put them all on baking trays lined with parchment paper. Cook in the preheated oven at 350º F for 30-40 minutes until crusty and fragrant.
3. Serve on vegan burger buns with your favorite toppings. You can also store them in the freezer in an airtight container and just reheat them when needed.

Tofu Stuffed Mushrooms Burgers

Mushrooms and tofu are a great meat substitute for vegans and the good news is, they taste amazing together, spiced with all sorts of condiments.

Servings: 4 burgers

Ingredients:
4 large, stuffing mushrooms
4 oz tofu
1 teaspoon soy sauce
1 green onion, chopped
1/2 teaspoon dried oregano
1/2 teaspoon dried basil
1/4 teaspoon dried rosemary
Salt, pepper

Directions:
1. Crumble the tofu in a bowl then stir in the green onion, oregano, basil and rosemary. Adjust the taste with salt and freshly ground pepper then scoop this mixture into the mushroom caps.
2. Arrange them on a baking tray and cook them in the preheated oven for 20-30 minutes until tender.
3. Serve the mushrooms on vegan burger buns with lettuce leaves for more freshness.

Lentil, Bean and Coriander Burgers

Lentils and beans are amongst the most commonly consumed basic ingredients in the vegan diet. Not only they are healthy, but they are also filling and rich in flavor.

Servings: 8-10 burgers

Ingredients:
2 cups cooked red lentils, drained
2 cups canned white beans, drained
1 onion, finely chopped
3 tablespoons sunflower seeds
1/2 cup rolled oats
1 teaspoon cumin
1/2 teaspoon dried oregano
1 tablespoon flax seeds, ground
2 tablespoons water
Salt, pepper

Directions:
1. Mix the flax seeds with water in a bowl and set aside to soak.
2. Put the white beans in a blender and process until a paste forms. Transfer into a bowl and stir in the cooked lentils, onion, seeds, oats, cumin and oregano, as well as the flax seeds. Taste and add salt and pepper as needed. Form small patties and arrange them on baking trays lined with parchment paper. Cook in the preheated oven at 350º F for 30-40 minutes or until crisp and golden brown on the surface.
3. Serve on vegan burger buns with your favorite toppings, such as tomatoes, lettuce leaves, or cucumber.

Summary

Thank you for reading my first book in the series: Quick and easy vegan recipes. I want to say thank you for the time you've invested in reading and preparing my recipes.

In this book, we've learned that there are dozens of ways to make vegan burgers. I recommend you to experiment with the methods of preparing burgers. Many people think burgers must be prepared on the grill or in a pan. But here we've learned that there are other wonderful ways and I think you should try them all. We've also learned that the preparation of burgers is not complicated and can even be easy and fun.

Now you too can enjoy a barbecue in the yard with your family and friends while enjoying a lot of wonderful recipes suitable for every occasion. I know from experience that if you continue this particular preparation of burgers, your whole family will follow a vegan diet because it tastes great and the energy gained from such a diet is just fantastic. Now, all that's left for you to do is to take action and implement the recipes in your home.

"101 healthy vegan burgers" is my contribution to a better world. I decided to read the series of books "Wisdom of the people" and, in my opinion, a collection of recipes in every book is a wonderful proof of the unique mutual support shared by vegans worldwide. My belief is that we all, together, can really make a difference in the world.

I also urge you—if you have a winning recipe- to send it to me, along with your picture, and I promise to publish it in one of my next books. Even if you do not have a recipe, you are invited to share with me your ideas or requests for future books in the series. Also I am always happy to receive reviews about my books and recipes, so do not hesitate to leave your reviews!

I hope I've contributed to you with my knowledge and experience. I wish you an abundance of love, health and happiness in your life.

Yours,

Daniel Nadav

ABOUT THE AUTHOR

I'm Daniel and I'm 33 years old and I've always considered myself a moral person. But I lived for many years with an internal dissonance--the lust for animal products collided with the heavy moral baggage eating them brought.

But, at 28, I woke up. The change was slow and not all at once but, one day, I could no longer fool myself and I realized that I must change my life--a Significant change. Then I went to Vipassana (meditation for 6 days in complete silence) and at the end of it I declared, "That's it, I'm vegan!"

When I came back from Vipassana I felt distressed. "I have no idea what I am going to eat today!" I do come from a cooking background (for many years I worked in diverse kitchens in my country), but my knowledge about vegan cooking was very poor. So I decided to contact members of our worldwide community through forums for vegans. I asked for recipes and tips and the response was amazing! I decided to leverage my passion for food to find the ultimate solutions for our community and began to write books of wonderful recipes for foods that I personally like the most...

My vision is to write a series of books consisting of original vegan recipes of my own--and of the members of the universal vegan community from around the world--and distribute them to as many people as possible. Each book will focus on one type of food and illustrate that there are dozens of ways to prepare it only from products of nature. The books incorporate original recipes that our wonderful community can enjoy and distribute, but they are also excellent for people who are not vegan but interested in Veganism and maybe a little afraid to make the change.

The series of books is my little contribution to a better world. I decided to read the "Wisdom of the people" series of books and, in my opinion, a collection of recipes in every book is a wonderful proof of the unique mutual support shared by vegans worldwide. My belief is that we all, together, can really make a difference in the world.

I also urge you--if you have a winning recipe you are welcome to send it to me, along with your picture and a picture of the recipe, and I promise to publish it in one of my next books. Even if you do not have a recipe, you are invited to share with me your ideas or requests for future books in the series.

For a much more harmonious, peaceful, balanced and sane life,

Daniel Nadav